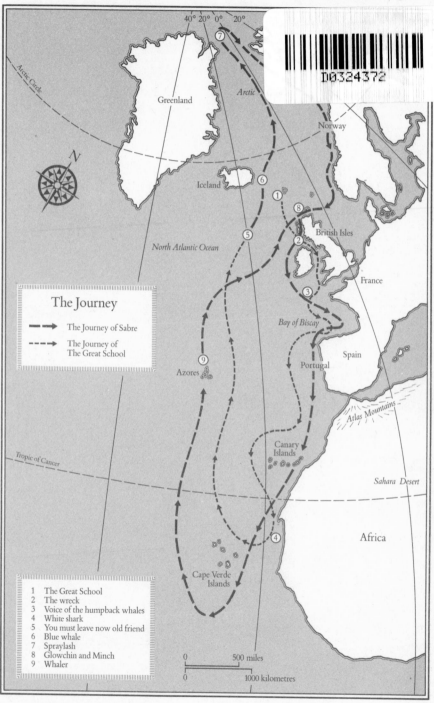

40° 20° 0° 20°

D0324372

Arctic Circle

Greenland

Arctic

Norway

N

Iceland

6

1

8

5

British Isles

2

France

North Atlantic Ocean

3

Bay of Biscay

Spain

Portugal

7

Atlas Mountains

The Journey

The Journey of Sabre

The Journey of
The Great School

9

Azores

Canary
Islands

Sahara Desert

Tropic of Cancer

4

Africa

Cape Verde
Islands

1   The Great School
2   The wreck
3   Voice of the humpback whales
4   White shark
5   You must leave now old friend
6   Blue whale
7   Spraylash
8   Glowchin and Minch
9   Whaler

0   500 miles

0   1000 kilometres

WHALE

#1644

WHALE

JEREMY LUCAS

JONATHAN CAPE
THIRTY BEDFORD SQUARE LONDON

First published 1981
© 1981 by Jeremy Lucas
Jonathan Cape Ltd, 30 Bedford Square,
London WC1

British Library Cataloguing in Publication Data

Lucas, Jeremy
Whale.
I. Title
823'.9'1F
ISBN 0 224 01921 X

Phototypeset by
Western Printing Services Ltd, Bristol
Printed in Great Britain by
St. Edmundsbury Press Ltd,
Bury St. Edmunds, Suffolk.

The chapter called Spraylash is for Katie, for she, without knowing how, made it the way it is. The rest is for my mother.

Contents

Introduction

GEOLOGICALLY SPEAKING HUMAN-KIND has not been here long: a mere flicker of time compared with the aeons that have passed since life was born in the primeval seas. Yet we have changed our world more than any other creature has found either necessary or possible. The big brain with its avalanching intelligence has, in the space of five million years, brought us from the timid bipedal apes who gingerly trod the forest-edged African Savannah, to modern man who has leapt, furiously and unconcernedly, far beyond the range and limits of any other animal. We have done so carelessly, seduced perhaps by the apparently infinite size and re-sources of our planet. We have tampered too long. We have driven hundreds of beasts to the brink of extinction and beyond. It is time to pay back the debt.

The whales have been here longer than we have, but we may well outlive them for they are one species that we have pushed to the very edge.

This is the story of a whale: *Orcinus Orca*, the Killer whale; his family, the creatures he meets and the environment in which he lives. It is not another horror story, where sharks and killer whales go berserk. It is a work of fiction that is at least possible, while much it contains is indeed fact. Its plausibility I leave to the imagination of the reader.

First Light

A BLACK-BACKED GULL beat low over the wave tops towards the land, which hung, purple and misty, on the eastern horizon. A hint of the morning sun appeared in the space between two of the far-off hills. The gull could hear the sounds of his own wings, and the endless slish slosh of the ocean rushing beneath him. He climbed higher above the surging water to inspect a wider area, now lit by the soft lilac of dawn.

Two shadows, side by side, stole across the surface. The waves parted, and two flashing backs humped into the air. Each back was armed with a fin, one much taller and straighter than the other. A sound, a sudden raucous blow, a deep cavernous shock of noise, rushed into the early morning sky as the whales spouted. The water vapour in their warm breaths condensed into shimmering rainbows and apparitions, swirling and dancing upon the sea. Then they were gone, and only the shadows crept on towards the sun.

Sabre was born that dawn. The shock of his cold Atlantic cradle caused him to take his first spluttering breath of the cool morning air, as Nightshadow, his mother, pushed him gently at the surface. The small swell rolled him, and the colours baffled him. Gradually his breathing became slower and stronger, and the waves rolled him less as he learned to move his flippers and flukes to compensate. His mother never left his side as they swam slowly towards the sound of far-off surf.

When Sabre was confident and relaxed his mother rolled over, exposing her soft white belly above the waves. Instinct drove him to feed from her, and his mouth filled with the rich milk. The cow whale waved her flipper at the sky and called to the calf, soothing him with her gentle reassuring voice.

The sounds of the sea were all around him, from the whisper of distant waves scrabbling at rock and cliff, to the wash of water each time he surfaced to blow. Sometimes there was a rushing noise as a shoal of fish fled to avoid the killer whales' approach: and always there was the voice of his mother, as warm as the milk she gave him, and as soft as the expanse of her belly. For fleeting moments another sound caught the baby whale's attention; the sound of his father, Orion, swimming close by, just out of visual range.

But Sabre was to remember nothing of the day of his birth. He did not recall his mother's gaze taking in his pure white belly and the smooth stark blackness of his back, his little hooked dorsal and the soft round tail and fins. Neither did he remember his father's surging swim as Orion protectively encircled them; nor even the brooding bulk of Scotland lying to the east beneath the sun's maternal glare.

The three killer whales spent the next few days in the same area, bathing in the last of the summer calm. They could taste a staleness in the tide twisting through the broad Sound. Flocks of petrels, shearwaters and fulmars flew in from the open ocean, darkening the face of the sea as they rested on the coast-line waters.

Each night the killers crept into the sea lochs, and

Sabre suckled ten gallons of milk, and listened to waves booming against the rocks. Spray on the wave tops shone under the moon, and lines of glowing foam reached in towards the shore. Life was very confusing and very happy.

They slept, Orion and the she-whale side by side, with Sabre in between: three blow-holes sighed into the Scottish air. The sounds of night willowed across the rocky floor; the surf rumbled on the beach, there was a splash somewhere across the bay, a lobster, deep in the sea, snapped closed a huge claw; old life was snatched away and new life prepared, after the halcyon ease of summer, for the cold slumber.

After three days and nights Sabre was strong enough for Orion to lead them back out into the tide races, and turn them towards the north.

The killer whales were in the wide sound of water that divides the mainland of Scotland from the Outer Hebrides: the North Minch. These were Sabre's home waters, an island-strewn pocket of the north eastern Atlantic; an area of rugged coast-lines, and a sea of ever changing mood and character. Sea birds flocked here, millions of them, and seals, porpoises and whales came to feed on the abundant fish shoals. Wherever the shoals collected, in the turbulent deep water, on the calm sand banks or the dark rocky floor, the hunters were never far away.

Soon the small family, Sabre, his mother and the big bull whale Orion, rounded Cape Wrath, the most north-westerly point of the Scottish mainland. Three miles out, well away from the heaving waves crashing against the Cape's rocks, they turned on to a more easterly course keeping parallel to the mainland, swimming slowly towards the Orkneys, more or less following the thirty fathom line.

While Sabre fed from his mother, Orion drove into the darkness below, in search of food for both himself and the cow whale waiting patiently on the surface with her little calf.

Sabre heard the strange noises of the hunt far below him; Orion's pulsing swim as he stole about on or near the sea floor; fast clicking or chirping noises that were his father's echo-locations; long quiet moans that were to tell Sabre's mother there was no danger, and that he was not far away. And sometimes there were the sounds of sudden death: the crunch of flesh and bone smashed against rock, or crushed between Orion's great jaws, tearing flesh, or just the sizzling sound of high speed swimming, and the kicking pulsating sprint as the bull whale gave chase. Cod and conger, ling and pouting, halibut and haddock; all met with the sudden focus of echo-locating sound that was the overture of death. In the inky darkness Orion sent them to oblivion.

He would appear suddenly from the gloom, his huge black and white shape scaring Sabre, until his mother's voice calmed him. Hanging in the bull's mouth would be some broken victim from the deep. Each one he presented to Sabre's mother. She swallowed all his gifts with an urgency that betrayed her hunger. She longed to dive with Orion, to hunt for herself, but Sabre was not yet ready for that. He could never travel far enough below the surface, or swim at the sustained high speeds necessary during a hunt. As he grew stronger the time would come, but meanwhile she could not leave the young whale to whimper and call for her, so she stayed by his side, and ate whatever her mate could bring her.

The coast of Scotland lay bathed in the autumn haze. The sea began to grow quiet as the fish shoals dispersed southwards. The birds followed, and each day the cliffs became less crowded. The cormorants sat above the water-line watching them go, oblivious to the changing season. The seals stayed on and collected together near the colony beaches, where their pups would be born before the acute cold of winter set in. The killer whales also remained, for the seals were careless at this time of year, and food was still abundant in the deep sea where temperatures changed little, and animals lived out their entire lives in the total darkness of their high-pressure world.

Orion would not leave these waters he knew so well, at least this year, for although times would be lean in the last months of winter, he would, with luck, be able to pull his family through until spring made life easy again.

Storm

THE WEATHER HAD steadily deteriorated all day.
Dawn had broken clear, too clear, and a cold
breeze began to ruffle the long Atlantic swell.
Soon the sky had hazed over with a veil of cirro-stratus,
and dark scuds of cloud rushed their warning towards the
east. By noon the sun was pale and weak; the sea had a
restless feel about it, and except for the wind there was
silence. The formerly frequent sonar noises of distant
porpoise schools were gone. The few remaining fish shoals
were silent and deep; immobile. Wing beats betraying
the urgency of its flight, an occasional gull hurried
towards the coast. Soon the birds had all disappeared,
and the bubbly living noises of the ocean were gone.
The latent inorganic savagery of a colossal bulk of
water remained, ominous and threatening. As enormous
banks of black cloud crowded in from the west, the
Atlantic hunched itself up in readiness. Abruptly, as
though it had never been there, the late autumn sun was
blacked out by the inverted anvil of the thunder-head
invading the sky. Beneath the pressing cloud lightning
forked into a now wind-crazed surface.

The whales were alone, climbing the white-veined
rollers, as the storm broke. Sabre, barely a week old,
swam between his parents. He started to blow more
frequently as he struggled up from the deep troughs. His
mother and Orion were in little danger, for they could

easily dive into the silent depths, and return to the surface only when the need for air demanded; but Sabre could not submerge for long, and he soon began to tire. His parents stayed with him, one each side, Orion up-wind each time they blew, protecting Sabre as much as possible. The tremendous weight of water pounded unheedingly across Orion's back, so that tons of grey water crashed upon Sabre, as he rolled and spun, gasping for air. His mother called to him, begging him to follow her, to dive, but her voice was lost in the fury. Nothing could be heard above the storm, as the wind churned up the water, and foam and spray hissed and leapt, clawing at the thick whale hide. What had been a long easy swell so little time ago, was now an ocean gone berserk.

Forgotten were the calms and breezes of summer. The light gales that had sped, fickle and boisterous, from the west, were mere adolescents with quick fiery tempers. Now autumn's adult had arrived; a precursor to winter. The Atlantic which had given life so easily, took it back. Gull, raven and hawk were ripped away from havens of rock and cliff, too carelessly chosen, with too little heed for the screaming winds that would tear across the Highlands and Islands. They were tossed about until they were no more than a broken bundle of feathers rolling over the sand, or caught in the heather. Here and there a seal lay where the waves had thrown it up against the rocks, like so much rubbish.

Even the sleek porpoises had their casualties as the schools ran headlong into each wave, shooting out from the other side like missiles. They searched for the protecting lee of some island, or the relative calm of a sea loch, but when they arrived so many friends were missing.

Each year the autumn gales arrived as a shock. Some

lasted a few hours, some a week. Always they left death
in their wake. Animals that should have moved south
sooner had stayed on, seduced by the golden sun. Others
should have moved to low ground and found warm
shelter in the moors, or climbed deeper into crevices in
the cliffs. For almost a month now the arrowheads of
birds littering the sky had gone. The deer were all off the
hills, and smoke wafted continuously from the chimneys
of shore-bound crofts. The mackerel shoals that had
crowded the summer seas had moved off to warmer
latitudes. Chasing the shoals were the sharks and dolphins, and many seals that could not wait for the herring
that would soon arrive. The signs of winter were there,
but each year some creatures were careless. The storms
and the cold snatched them all away, finally clearing the
land, sea and air for winter's grip.

The whales were caught this time far out in the open
sea. The nearest land was the island sprawl of Orkney,
and it was towards this they headed. Miles down wind
the islands lay in the path of the storm, pulverised by the
mountainous seas.

From every direction seals and porpoises, dolphins
and whales, fisherman and warship converged on the
islands, all striving towards the multi-entranced bowl of
water that is the safe heart of the Orkneys: Scapa Flow.

While night fell unnoticed the storm reached its cli-
max. The sloping seas were etched by bizarre patterns, lit
by lightning flashes and the eerie glow of phosphorescent
foam and spray. Sabre was completely exhausted, rely-
ing entirely on his parents. Occasionally a freak wave
would appear. Formed by combination between two
waves, the resultant mammoth would climb slowly, so
slowly, skyward, and then, with not enough energy to

roll, would collapse, and tons of water would crash down upon the whales struggling at the surface.

Nightshadow grew tired, and began to rely more and more on Orion's great strength. The water's surge would drag her away from Sabre, and she would be lost in the deep troughs. Searching in panic in the lashing rain and walls of spray, she would find them each time, as a brief white flash revealed Orion, incredibly holding Sabre in his mouth above the waves, the water foaming about him, as if he were a solid rock jutting defiantly from the sea.

Between them Sabre's parents fought through the night to keep him safe. The first grey pall of dawn found the whales in Hoy Sound heading for Bring Deeps, between Graemsay and Hoy, and the shelter of the Flow. Already they were leaving the wind-whitened wildness behind them, as the tide pushed them through the Deeps.

Slowly, as if awakening from exhausted sleep, Sabre became aware that it was over. He could hear his mother's voice again, and there was a saner rhythm about the waves. He could breathe more easily, and push his own way through the banking seas. The horrors of the night had gone. The cruel Atlantic had been merciful this once.

All morning, while Orion hunted ravenously in the plentiful waters of the Flow, Sabre drank gallon after gallon of milk, and set aside for the moment the knowledge, learnt so young, of what the Atlantic could do.

Learning

THEY PASSED Flotta and Ronaldsay in the night. A late October mist welcomed the whales as they crept into the Pentland Firth, leaving behind them the becalmed waters of the Flow. Each time they surfaced the sounds of their blow were borne on the mist far across the stillness of the Firth.

Two seals lay wallowing on the surface, drifting where the tide took them. Vertical in the water, only their noses poked above the mirror-calm face of the sea. Slowly they sank, asleep, until a faint awareness of tightness in their chests made them waft their hind flippers to push themselves upwards.

When Orion heard their echo he was not far from them. Soundlessly his dorsal slid away, and he descended straight down to a hundred feet, just off the sea floor. His vision told him nothing, for at that depth there was not the slightest suggestion of light; but his ears fed him all the information he needed. With his sonar he located the seals above him, turned upwards, and kicked.

Perfectly shaped, and powered for tremendous acceleration, he hit the surface with such speed that he shot high in the air, carrying with him one of the seals, already dead, before it could wake from its fatal slumber. Momentum and the force of gravity grappled for the whale's immense body. For a second Orion hung there motionless, before dropping back, tail first, into the sea.

The explosion of his attack rumbled across the Firth; sea birds nestling, head under wing, on their beds of rock or water, were startled into flight. Killer whales were about, and hunting. High in the sky, and far away, they would be safe.

The other seal survived. Twice she was almost caught, in a chase that ended on the shallows of Swona Isle, where the killer whale dared not swim for fear of becoming beached. She dodged him once in the clear open water, while the air was still fresh in her lungs. She hid from his sonar amongst the weeds and rocks of the sea bed, until her lungs forced her up into the open, where Orion found her again. While she gulped air he closed in, but even as his dorsal swept down she veered off, and summoning the maximum power that her tearing muscles could give her, and ignoring the mounting dizziness in her head, she bolted for the island. In the end it was the reefs that saved her, for while she could swim over the sharp fingers of rock, Orion was forced to pass round them: and then she was above the sand, and the killer whale gave up the chase.

Weakly the seal pulled herself up on to the beach, where she collapsed into a disturbed sleep. Throughout the day, while the mist slowly cleared, she dreamt of the white teeth closing over her head. One moment she was chasing flounders on the sun-drenched sandy shallows, and the next the light was cut off, as a killer whale's shadow passed overhead. When she awoke in the late afternoon she stared out over the reefs, and saw the menacing black fin appear now and then, and it was not alone. Two more fins, smaller and curved, shone briefly in the sun a little farther out to sea: but now she was not afraid, she could stay on the beach until they left.

Thus Sabre's introduction to life was spent in the harsh northern seas. During the long winter that followed Orion took them as far north as the Shetland Isles, and as far south as Mull in the Inner Hebrides. Sabre watched his parents hunt seals and porpoises, or followed them down to the wrecks and reefs on the sea floor, where they took cod and squid, lobster and conger eels; anything that would satisfy their huge appetites for another winter day. Sabre was spared the scavenging and the hunting. He just filled his increasingly demanding belly with milk whenever his mother would allow.

The killer whale calf grew quickly, so that soon even the most violent seas bothered him little, and caused his parents no concern for his safety.

Sometimes they rested and drifted with the currents: more often they swam in the bull's wake towards new hunting grounds; towards the ever fainter sounds and smells of potential prey. Their lives became governed by the dwindling food supplies, as the northern cold intensified.

Sometimes accidentally, sometimes with lethal purpose, the killers crossed the paths of other wanderers. From these meetings Sabre learnt of the many and strange creatures with which he shared the sea. These were times of rapid learning, while Orion and Nightshadow killed whatever they found alive, and ate the few victims of winter left floating on the sea.

With the warm waters of the Gulf Stream acting as a feeble buffer to the currents seeping down from the north, the whale's appetites could barely be satisfied in an ocean where only the strong and wary had learnt to survive during these cold winter months. Orion was the hunter and nothing else: in an ocean just above freezing point there was no time for anything else.

One day it might be a shoal of cod, revealed as a muzzy return wave to Orion's sonar. Fifty feet down, just above the twilight region of the ocean, the killer whales would meet echelon after echelon of the dark shapes swimming slowly south towards warmer seas. After a summer's feeding in the waters from northern Norway to Greenland the cod were sleek and muscular. The killer whales harvested the shoals, gorging themselves with the protein drifting on its migration south. Another day it would be huge conger eels, snatched from their lairs, as they skulked, python-like, amongst the reefs and cracks on the sea-bed. And then there would be empty days: days when Sabre's mother grew ravenous, and Orion impatient: long days, and even longer nights, when there was nothing; except perhaps a seagull or a puffin, that had been disdainfully unaware of Orion's closing shadow. Sometimes a whole week would pass before Orion could lead them to prey, maybe a seal or dolphin caught in the open water. In the times of hunger they were reduced to scavenging from the floor. Perhaps they would be lucky, when a storm left carcasses tossing in the waves. Usually they were not so lucky, and Orion hunted continuously, investigating and analysing anything that might be food. Therefore Sabre's world was a hard one: the bitter cold had to be beaten back at the expense of some other living creatures: the killer whale's prey.

There were times when hunting was impossible, when the water turned white and steep, with the harsh, blizzard-laden wind reaching for them amongst the deep valleys between the waves. They rode out the storms, spouting in the troughs, before the mountains of water passed over their backs. But the wild times were often their allies. Seeking sanctuary from the endless noise of the open sea amongst the sea-lochs of the Scottish Islands, they would stumble upon other creatures resting in the calm.

On clear nights, when the moon shone fiercely in the frozen sky, Sabre watched the stars. Copying his father's vertical attitude on the surface, he poked his head up into the crisp air, and gazed at the planets and stars, slipping almost imperceptibly towards the eastern horizon. The distant lights became Sabre's friends. He was soon able to recognise them and came to distinguish one from another with the certainty born of long observation. There was Sirius, the dog star, bright and twinkling, often trailing a short tail of half-imagined green as it stole across its zenith. He could see the hunter constellation, Orion, sword held tightly in his three white-star belt, marching in dominant fashion through the night. And there was the Plough, pointing Sabre to the Pole Star, hanging low on the northern horizon. One day this star would draw Sabre on his journey to the ice; but that was far away in the future, and for now he was happy merely to stand upright in the water at his father's side, watching the sparkling canopy through the night. So Sabre learnt to navigate by the stars, in his first lesson-strewn winter.

He learnt too of man, or man's machines. He heard the high-pitched whirring of propeller blades, and the low rumble of heavy engines; the shouting of fishermen across the calms, and the crash and rattle of their nets and buoys as they set about their work. Occasionally after a careless crewman had fallen asleep on the job there was the foul taste of oil, and the smell of decay and death in the sea.

In the mid-day light they found the shoals of herring fry. Moving in one amoeboid mass, the tiny fish might be bunched into a heavy cloud, or stretched out, eel-like, as far as the killer whales' eyes could see. Each individual fish aligned itself with its neighbours, obeying the invisible, but total, discipline of the shoal: a homogeneous mass diffusing into the grey distance, became, in a flash of silver, a solid mirror, impenetrable and dazzling. The only rule-breakers were the weak, the dying and the dead, left twinkling in the shoal's wake, an insignificant waste amongst the infinity of numbers that survived.

Hour after hour the whales gorged themselves, harvesting until they could eat no more. Each mouthful created a hole, but even as it formed the silver bodies flowed into the gap, and as though nothing had happened, the shoal continued its wave-like motion upon the tide.

It would continue like this for years, as the herring slowly grew. Always the same enormous numbers, and always hunters looming out of the distance. Changing predators with the changing seasons, but each and all filling his belly. And in the end came the nets, enveloping and concentrating them, closing irresistibly around them, until the millions became thousands. A few of these, a very few, survived, left with the charge of reproducing the unimaginable numbers, so that it could all begin again.

To Sabre it appeared that the feast had done nothing to the shoal. There was still the cloud of fish stretching away into the murk. The only difference was, that after each attack, hundreds of twinkling bodies fell away, like glowing rain, into the half-light.

Finally, stomachs full, the whales watched the herring disappear into the greyness of evening. Sometimes they found the shoals the following day, but usually they lost them, and the search for new prey would begin.

Slowly the winter ate itself out. The days grew longer, and the ocean warmer, especially in the shallows and in the estuaries. The rocks became clothed in green, and hidden amongst the interwoven leaves wafting in the tide, the animals felt the new warmth, and began to stir. Spring thrust its way into the sea, and the killer whales took advantage of easier life at last. Now it was not mere survival; the winter sleep was broken.

Summer

THE BURST OF spring reached into the darkest, coldest corners, loosening winter's hold. Hunting became easier for the whales, as the ocean breathed again. The lessons of the harsh winter months were replaced by sun-swept days and calm nights, filled with sounds of life.

The mackerel shoals swam northwards, chased by summer's visitors to the high latitudes. The tope and blue shark arrived, materialising, sleek and deadly, torpedo shaped, and quick-jawed. The big sharks were not far behind: fat, wicked-faced porbeagles and mako, and stealing out of the gloom, fierce and fast, a lone thresher shark whose tail, as long as its body, swept the beast on its migration north.

The air filled with skeins and flocks of birds, flying up and away from the white heat of Africa, and the sultry humidity of southern Europe. A luckless few fell into the waves, incapable of completing the mammoth journey, but most made it, and more followed until the islands of the temperate seas were filled with their chatter, as they fluttered and dipped upon the waves, glad to have escaped the oppressive heat of the mid-Atlantic, and the burnt out reaches of the Sahara.

Sabre watched, and heard them all arrive. He watched Orion chasing away the sharks and, with chin above the waves, saw the falcons ending their long stoop as, in a flutter of feathers, another summer visitor fell victim to their talons beneath the cliffs.

During the warm months the calf whale was weaned from his mother's milk. He began to take the silver-grey mackerel, chasing them down into the dark regions, or snapping at them, as they jumped and skittered along the surface. At first he was a clumsy hunter, hopelessly inefficient, carelessly allowing the green shapes to slide past, learning slowly, with nonchalant summer abandon. Orion brought him scraps of red meat, and fins from sharks that had dared to come too close, while gradually Sabre became more proficient with his own fishing.

While Orion was far below hunting for squid on the sea floor, and Sabre chased mackerel into the teeming seas, the challenger appeared, big, and black, and confident. Gliding silently down a wave on outstretched flippers, he rode down towards Nightshadow and plunged beneath her, oblivious to all save her rounded female shape; but as he turned towards her she kicked, and called out urgently for Orion.

The intruder was a young bull killer whale, who had been alone since being exiled from his own family pod off the coast of Norway. He had spent the last summer amongst the fjords, tasting the fresh water from the glaciers, and feeling nothing under his belly but the colossal deep. He grew lonely, and set off across the Norwegian sea in search of others of his kind, calling, hoping, all through the winter. Spring had found him still alone, off the Sutherland coast of Scotland. He continued his search until, miraculously, one day, under the summer sun, he found her; the beautiful cow whale, alone with her calf on the seascape.

He had not heard Orion, for had he done so he would never have dared to approach. He was startled as Sabre's mother turned and fled into the seas, screaming out her anger.

Sabre was there first, instinct driving him to bare his teeth and lunge towards the bull. There was a thud, and the surface shook. Sabre backed off and prepared to attack again, but the Scandinavian's flukes lashed round and caught the calf in the face, stunning him for his insolence.

When Orion heard the terror in Nightshadow's voice he shot away from the sea floor towards her, thrusting up to the light, towards the danger. By the time he reached the twilight region he heard Sabre's attack, and against the mirrored surface saw the big bull, mouth opening, flukes churning: moving towards the calf.

Abruptly the intruder became aware of Orion hurtling up from the deep. Even as he turned away the enormous weight crashed into him, lifting and rolling him, and forcing the air from his lungs; and then he felt the teeth tearing at his flesh, as together the whales spun and grappled in the spray.

Twice Orion cleared the water, and falling upon his challenger, sunk his teeth into the Norwegian's thick hide. But at the first chance Orion gave him the young bull bolted, leaving a thin red line in his wake. His mistake learnt he did not return, but turned for the north, and began his search again; calling, hoping . . .

At first it was just a small black ripple, with a trembling black centre, skating across the surface. It grew, until it became a shining black triangle a yard high and as wide at the base where it met the submarine-like body. The fin continued moving, forming a gentle bow-wave, which sparkled in the sun as it rolled across the silky surface. The tip of another fin appeared, twenty feet astern of the first, and it too grew, until it was a tall glistening sail waving gently to and fro, as it powered the basking shark across the sunlit sea.

Both fins belonged to the same fish, as it travelled, huge mouth agape, sifting plankton over its gill-rakers. Like the baleen whales, the basking shark had grown to its monstrous size on the tiniest food in the sea. It was totally adapted to its life as harvester, with its cavernous mouth, and lines of teeth arrayed to act as filters for endless acres of water passing over the gill arches.

Singly, or in shoals of up to a hundred beasts, the sharks sweep across the sea, governed solely by the floating pastures.

The shark that appeared out of the jade-green distance, was following the plankton bloom that reached into the north under the June sun. The whales heard the basking shark long before they saw it, and while Orion swam off to investigate the new threat, Sabre and his mother listened, as the mottled grey-brown fish drew nearer.

In front of Orion the four-ton giant entered their circle of visibility. Apparently oblivious to the presence of the killer whales it waved its tail, thrusting on through the plankton soup. The whales swam out of the shark's path, and listened to the water rushing through the cleft-like gills, and watched as the shark's shadow lanced down into the haze cutting across the deep.

They followed the gentle giant, mezmerised by its lazy progress. Sabre swam close to his father's side, awed, and a little frightened. He had never seen anything so big before, though it showed no hint of aggression.

After gliding in the shark's wake until the sun was sinking, Sabre's curiosity overcame his fear. Before his parents could head him off, he leapt forward, and bit hard into the shark's tail. The water churned, and Sabre was thrown clear, as, in a welter of foam, the fish submerged.

Nightshadow slapped at Sabre's mouth with her foreflippers, chiding him for his stupidity. His mouth was full of a bitter viscous fluid, part of the shark's antiparasite defence. Blood oozed from the calf's mouth, his tongue badly scratched by the rough skin of the shark.

High above, soaring with out-stretched wings on the soft zephyrs of summer, the keen-eyed gulls watched for fish shoals. Their attention was attracted by the sudden crash of spray. They cried out in alarm as the huge brown shape fell away into the deep, leaving the three whales on the surface; the only creatures marring the otherwise placid mirror that stretched away beneath them all the way to the clear curve of the horizon.

Later the shark returned to the surface, drawn by the abundant food lying there. It had already forgotten the incident with the foolish calf whale. As the sun fell the fish again started to submerge, until it was just a small ripple with a trembling dark centre.

The time of the salmon came to the Scottish seas. Speeding down in a shoaled surge from the Arctic circle, the lilac-backed fish crowded towards the shore, tasting for the peat-laden waters of the rivers of their birth. Waiting for a spate they collected in the bays and estuaries of their rivers. Far inland a heavy summer shower on the high heather moors was enough to lift the rivers, and draw the salmon home. The long swim up to the shallows, to the breeding reds, began in the bays, as the first taste of peat drifted out to sea.

A young dog otter trod, soft pawed, upon the sun-baked rocks. A trail of water marked his passage up from the bladder-wrack, lying dark and dull, exposed by the ebb tide. At the water's edge was the body of a salmon. From the flanks of the silver carcass neat mouthfuls of flesh had been torn away. The otter had left the rest for the eager gulls, already on their way across the bay. In these times of plenty the otter could afford to be generous. He had only to slip back into the waves, allow his tail to drive him out into the blue water, and his next quick-finned meal would appear. Now, in the heavy afternoon sun, the otter had filled his belly. He climbed upon a big boulder with a good view of the area, and sniffed at the air. Content that there was no danger he fell into an easy sleep, waiting for the salmon to be driven into the shallows by the changing tide.

Fleetingly, far out in the bay, a fin appeared, and a gust of vapour shimmered above the surface. Two more fins shone quickly across the quiet waters. The gulls saw the flashes and filed the information away in their quick brains. The dog-otter slept while the killer whales moved in with the tide.

The salmon had drawn the whales from far out at sea. Through the night Orion's sonar had constantly clicked, while he led his family towards the sound of surf. At dawn they had all stood upright in the water, and seen the cliffs reaching high above the white flecked swell. Orion took them along the coast, avoiding the ragged teeth of the reefs. At noon they found the bay, and heard the hiss of another shoal of salmon crowding towards the river.

The whales swept in over the sandy bed, leaving a

yellow wake puffing and swirling in the eddies. Above them were the echelons of salmon, forming, in places, an almost solid ceiling. At Orion's command the three whales lifted towards the pale bellies, and the feast began.

Being close to the surface the fish leapt high in the air as the killer whales rushed into them. In the afternoon sun the silver bodies of the salmon reflected the golden glow, and appeared as flames leaping from the calm waters. Falling back, their writhing bodies were snatched into merciless, ravenous jaws.

In abandon the whales leapt with the fish: devils cart-wheeling and dancing in the flames, bellies fiery pink, backs shining and dark, and the big dorsals slicing the air, they crashed back amongst the salmon.

With a twitch the otter awoke. He rose on his hind paws, and whiskers bristling, stared at the killers. Each time the whales leapt a crash resounded around the bay. The otter yickered and snarled, and with an anxious motion, ran backwards and forwards over his rock. Presently the whales stopped jumping, and the otter again settled down to sleep.

He awoke in the evening to the sound of a light breeze rippling the waters of the bay. He had forgotten the bad dream of the killer whales, and bounced down to the waves, his stomach gurgling for attention. His tail quickly pushed him away from the swaying weeds, and his sharp eyes searched beneath the dappled waves for salmon.

He half saw, half imagined the black shape, and an angry gash of teeth. He turned in a twisting, life-saving burst of energy, and fled, arrow straight, for the shallows. He reached safety bare moments before Sabre could strike. The killer whale stopped, his belly scraping over the sand, and waves washing over his back. The otter continued his flight until he was far up the river, and listening to the chuckling water run over the age-smoothed rocks. Here beneath the wooded banks of his river, he was safe.

The easy days of summer drew on until the first of the September gales marked the changing season, and long spear-headed flights of birds winged towards the south. As abruptly as they had appeared the mackerel and salmon were gone, and big head-seas from the north reminded the killer whales that the calm transience of summer was a fleeting luxury that was quickly fading.

Sabre, now a year old, pushed unconcernedly through the banking waves. The green water rolled down his broad back. On either side of him, his mother and Orion called quietly, and he sang back into the tumbling seas.

It had been a kind summer; a fat and warm summer, and surely life must always be like this?

Death of a Hunter

T HE CROFTER WAS a man no longer young, who
had grown tired of the crazy mainland life. He
now lived with his wife on Seal Island, a desolate
outpost on the edge of the Outer Hebrides. From spring
to autumn the couple worked calmly, but hard, with
their handful of sheep, a cow and two collies. The dogs,
like the man and his wife, were old and rested more than
worked; but together they scratched a living from the
island.

In the winter they worked in the short daylight hours
on their snow-swept landscape, and then huddled
together in front of the constantly glowing warmth of
the peat in the hearth, while outside the night's fury
battered at the defiant stonework of their croft.

They lived in the summer, they survived in the winter,
and together they grew old in the quiet Highland happiness.

While walking the island the crofter often stared out
across the blue ocean. Stared with those pale blue eyes of
the highlander, that appear to have gazed forever into the
distance. He looked for seals. He thought his life was like
that of a seal. He and they it seemed were both creatures
on the edge of survival, outcasts in a world of different
things, different values. He often sat watching them play
in the waves, or hunt amongst the island's reefs for their
prey.

For this was a collecting place for seals; a haven in the blue water. They could haul out and rest here after long hazardous ocean treks or feeding sprees.

As winter prepares to grasp the north the beaches come alive with breeding colonies of Grey seals. Out of the pounding waves of September come the first heavy seal cows. They haul themselves above the stinging spray and select warm little hollows in the sand by the rocks, and under sheltering overhangs. They find places where the sun-baked stones of summer will warm the calves for their first few vulnerable days.

As usual the crofter watched the seals collect. Mainly cows in the first week, and then a few big bulls. Each bull, a beach master, patrolled his own section of beach where his harem had collected. He guarded his section with water-cascading violence. Any late-arriving cow, and these were many, was ushered by one of the bulls into his kingdom, and with this angry simplicity she became his.

Soon the places offering the most shelter were all occupied, and the late arrivals had to make do with the open beach, where they scooped out shallow hollows in the white shingle, and then lay awaiting the impending birth of their pups. In their watery eyes was a sense of impatience, and sometimes a hint of pain, and the occasional tremor of their bodies, or sudden shake of the head, told its own story. They would not have long to wait.

Within two weeks the beach was crowded and noisy, the bark and the noise of the bulls adding to the constant crash and hiss of the surf.

The first pups arrived. Their mothers licked at their bloody coats until they were yellow. The whimpering little seals snuggled into their mother's soft warm flanks, where they found comfort and milk. Within hours of their birth the rain, the wind-driven spray, the wind itself, and their mothers' constant attention, had turned their coats from a yellow matted mess into a fluffy white tinged with blue.

The wind was cold from the north. The nights were bitter, cold rain and hail sizzling on the rocks and in the sea. In the mornings the briskly running clouds sped away, so that the calves basked and slept on the sun-warmed sands. After the youngsters had finished their breakfasts of the fatty yellow milk, their mothers lolloped weakly down to the surf to clean themselves, and take the weight off their aching bodies. They fished a while in a vain attempt to satisfy their raging appetites. Soon they hurried back to their whimpering calves who were gazing pathetically, longingly, over the beach, searching for the warm dark shape that had deserted them. The seal colonies thus grew over the next few weeks, until the beach was littered with many fluffy white pups, whose mewing filled the autumn air.

Then the killer whales arrived.

On the northern shore of the island the crofter came to see the seals each morning before his chores called him away. From a rock that offered a clear view of his favourite beach he watched the seals playing and feeding, and marvelled at the sudden explosive battles of rival males. One morning he was disturbed by a lifeless brown shape rolling about in the tide-line, being crushed and battered by the waves. It was the corpse of a cow seal. Each year the rigours imposed by birth take their toll, and many cubs also die, but this corpse distressed him because it was headless; and an ugly wound ran down the exposed belly where the flesh had been torn away.

The man immediately thought of sharks, but it was getting late in the year for the blue sharks that came every summer, chasing the mackerel shoals to the north. He dismissed this, and imagined the seal had fallen prey to one of the conger eels that skulked about the island's reefs. He never thought of the killer whales that regularly passed the island a mile to the west, usually hidden by the mountainous winter seas.

The next morning, however, he arrived just in time to see one of the bulls come surging out of the waves and haul itself weakly on to the sand. It lay there with its flanks heaving, while the water broke over it. After gasping at the air for ten minutes the bull pulled himself painfully up the beach, followed by a vivid red trail, vulgar and stark against the white sand. It was then that the man noticed that part of the seal's hind flipper was missing. Blood oozed freely from the wound.

The way the bull had dashed on to the beach, desperately out of breath, suggested that it had been chased. The crofter turned his attention to the sea. On the bank of a wave, where the green water began to take a deeper hue, his stare became held by a dark swirling patch. Abruptly the disturbance grew until the man could begin to see shape. Then, amidst a burst of spray, a seal was launched skyward. It rolled, as if in slow motion, over and over as it fell back towards the vast form beneath. Momentarily a black flash showed above the wave. In the same half-imagined moment the seal and the hunter were gone, leaving barely a mark upon the surface. And then, for the first time, the crofter saw Orion clearly. Heading towards the beach the killer whale blew, his dorsal fin rolling and slicing down into his own bow-wave. Closer and closer to the beach he surged, until the man was sure that the big black whale's belly must have been scraping along the shingle. Orion blew again, his spout sounding savage and defiant above the wind. At last, back exposed, the killer whale turned and headed out to sea. The crofter stared after him, and then noticed that the dark shape was now flanked by two smaller shadows. The warrior returning home, rejoicing with the spoils of war.

The crofter stood there a long while, his hair blowing wildly in the wind, his gaze fixed upon the retreating whales. Finally he turned away and made for home, his eyes suddenly dark beneath a fixed, thoughtful frown.

That night he sat unmoving, staring into the glowing peat embers. He was remembering stories of Grampus, or killer whales, from his days on the mainland. He knew that the island's new visitors were these killers; whales that ate seals and porpoises, herding and slaughtering the poor beasts against the rocks and cliffs of the Western Isles. The fishermen had always said that the killer whales were a mixed blessing. They would kill many seals that would otherwise do much damage to nets and fish shoals. But on the other hand the fishermen were terrified of the Grampus. They would never take a small boat out when killers were known to be about. And there were other stories too, darker tales of many years ago. Tales that most people thought were just fishermen's tales, tales of death; people being killed by the Grampus. The crofter frowned, and then fell asleep hoping the killers would not return.

A storm rose in the night. The next morning found the crofter bent into the wind at his vantage point above the beach, staring out over the white-capped sea. The whales could be anywhere out there, hidden in the deep troughs.

He glanced at the seals. They were all huddled in their hollows and rock shelters, high above the reaching fingers of the mounting seas.

He had not seen the whales, but somehow he knew they were still there. Somewhere out there beneath the tortured surface he knew the dark shapes would be lurking, waiting, riding out the storm, and then death would swim again amongst the seals.

The wind rose still more through the day, and darkness came early, while rain and hail lashed the sparse heather moors. The free-roaming sheep huddled together in the few sheltered places the island afforded. The crofter spent a restless night, listening to the storm batter at the window, and the wind scream in the chimney. The cow seals on the beach sheltered their vulnerable weeping calves as best they could, but even so three fluffy white corpses shone in the dawn.

With daybreak the storm died. The clouds rushed away to the south, leaving only small dark scuds in their wake. The crofter rose an hour after the sun. After a quick breakfast he rushed down to the shore. He saw the killers immediately and his heart sank. The menacing black fins rose out of the swell one by one. He could see every detail in the fresh clear air. Having already fed, Orion was leading his family away from the beach. The surf driving up on to the sand was coloured here and there with red. The adult seals were barking loudly, and staring anxiously out to sea in the direction of the rolling black backs.

The crofter sat down and watched the whales disappear amongst the rolling hills of water. He felt powerless, but he knew that somehow he had to destroy the killers, or drive them away, before they drove away the seals, before they destroyed the shores of his island.

So he made his plan.

The next day he arrived at the rock which was his vantage point an hour before dawn, setting out his kit by the icy light of the moon.

Dawn crept into the eastern sky as the moon sank into the ocean to the north-west. The stars were gradually extinguished by the greyness that sketched its ghostly way across the sky. There was not a breath of wind, but the air was penetratingly cold. The brooding Atlantic rolled away in a long easy swell in front of him. The only sound in the otherwise silent half-light was the gurgling water, as it weaved its way amongst the rocks and over the shingle.

A splash of orange now tinted the east, and extending shafts of brighter light promised the coming of the sun. The crofter shivered, the sunburst oddly exaggerating the cold. The combination of silence, light, and the dawn cold, made him feel very isolated and lonely, somehow lost. He wished that he could be warm and snug in bed. But he had a job he must do. He pulled his blanket tight around his neck and looked out over the sombre, heavy ocean, but saw no comfort there, nor any threat, only the rolling hypnotic swell. The comfort of sleep beckoned and the crofter began to forget his purpose.

A bird called, and startled the man out of his doze. It was a single gull somewhere in the sky to his left, climbing up to be first to herald the dawn. Looking up in the direction of its piercing call, the crofter saw the gull's belly glowing dull red against the sun, not yet showing above the horizon. Scanning the sea, now beginning to show a hint of very deep blue, the man again saw nothing but water. His gaze took in the beach. Looking like sacks washed up by the previous tide, he saw the seals all motionless in their sleep. Strung out along the beach there were perhaps fifty in all.

The sun cut above the horizon and flooded the Hebrides with its warm light, revealing all the yellowing autumn colours, as both land and sea prepared for winter.

More gulls were calling now, and flying from their night's perch to find some morning mischief, and perhaps a scrap of breakfast. The seals began to stir, and the crofter watched as the baby seals nuzzled closer to their mothers' flanks.

In the wave tops just off the beach he noticed the head of a big bull Grey seal pop up now and then to eye his harem. He was a beach master up early for some quiet fishing. He was alert for any rival male who might steal out of the sea in a full-blooded attempt to get among the females. The master bull was not alert, however, for more definite, more lethal danger.

Orion was approaching from the direction of the sun, and was thus hidden against the dazzling sky. He was swimming very fast, parallel to the beach, no more than a hundred yards off. With the tide flooding he felt safe from becoming stranded in the relatively shallow water. Searching far out in the open water to the north the crofter failed to notice Orion's deadly approach. The whale was completely submerged for the last four hundred yards of his attack as he closed on the beach. Even the gulls failed to cry the alarm as the shadow sped in for the kill.

The beach master was chasing flounders away from the sandy shallows into deeper rocky water, where he twisted around the rocks in pursuit of the escaping flatfish, whose wake of disturbed sand marked their path. Engrossed by his own hunt the seal saw the white flash much too late. In the same heart-wrenching moment he felt the sudden pressure of water, and sensed the presence of something huge and deadly. Long ago he had been surprised by a devil-faced Mako shark in warmer seas off Cornwall. With sharp turns, all manner of twisting and turning, he had managed to escape that encounter, and had even nipped away a piece of the shark's dorsal fin. But here was something different. The killer whale's brain is not the puny sense receptor of a shark; it is a calculating mammalian brain: even so there would have been a chance if Orion had not been moving so fast.

The bull seal rolled and pushed himself towards the beach, but even as he took his first, and last, powerful kick, the whale was upon him. In a rocky corridor of water, barely two fathoms deep, Orion's sweeping dorsal fin slammed into the seal's side, spinning him around, smashing the air from his crushed lungs. And then the whale's great flukes swept up beneath the helpless beach master, hurling him high into the air in a cloud of spray. The seal performed the most dramatic motion of his life, but he was dead before he fell back into the waves.

The crofter stared in disbelief. So fast! It had all been so incredibly fast! One minute he had been staring at a smooth tilting surface unmarked by anything, except an occasional gull preening nonchalantly, itself unaware of the danger so close, and then ... Then the unimaginable! The smooth water, the explosion of white, the dark shape shooting into the sky, and the bucking mammoth beneath it all. The man saw the details of the kill with sickening awesome clarity; the mocking black flukes waving above the churning water, even as the brown bundle that was the broken remains of the seal fell back towards them.

The silent autumn dawn was abruptly transformed into a chaos of terrifying sound. The gulls rose screeching into the air, huge waves were thrown against the rocks. The seals all lurched into their peculiar side-hopping motion, and barked as one, from the safety of the beach.

Orion gulped down the seal and waited. He waited, blissfully unaware of the noisy rebuke from his victim's wives upon the beach, and uncaring of the gulls circling overhead. He would wait while the bubbles caressed his body, until the disturbance he had created settled, and then he would begin the hunt again and kill a seal for his family waiting to seaward. He waited while the slow swell washed over his back, and the golden sun dappled on the white sand beneath him.

At first the crofter just crouched by his rock, incapable of movement, and merely held his breath, appalled and overawed. But then it occurred to him, through the haze of violence, that this was his chance. The moment he had planned, the moment he had hoped for. Now it was here it was somehow unreal, impossible. He lifted the gun very slowly. It was a heavy, old gun, a 0.44 calibre that had been used for stags back in his mainland days. He stared along the sights as another wave washed gently over Orion's back. Like a stationary submarine the whale just wallowed in the swell. And then he started forward, and in that movement his back nudged above the surface. Orion, in a carefree glow of triumph after the intense joy of his kill, began to turn. The man's finger closed over the trigger as he watched the dark shape inch over the sand. He could see every detail in the now clear water, even the white splash behind the whale's eye.

The huge rounded flippers wafted gently to and fro. Quietly the immense dorsal lifted high above the waves, followed by the back and the smooth round head; and then even the white splash poked above the surface.

The brief, trigger-squeezing moment changed everything. The rifle's crash was stunning in its intensity: an alien, evil sound in a peaceful Hebridean isle.

The seals on the beach kicked up sand in their panic. Many rushed for the sea, ignoring the threat of the killer whale. Others repeatedly circled their calves, barking insistently and continuously, not knowing what to do, not understanding this new threat. The gulls again rose screaming into the air. A falcon, making a plummeting dive on a rock-dove over the moor, suddenly met the shock wave, broke off his attack, and fled for the sanctuary of his eyrie in the cliffs not far away.

A surge of water had been passing over Orion's back as the bullet struck. A column of white shot into the air, but the water was a flimsy shield. It was not enough. The bullet slammed and exploded in the whale's neck, boring through the blubber as if it did not exist. Then two vertebrae splintered. The fragments of bone and lead tore through the upper part of his body, causing agony in their travel. Some pierced a lung, and the pain flooded uncontrollably over his entire body. He jerked convulsively, his tail flukes lashing for the very last time above the waves. Releasing the air he had taken in on his last blow in one long, drawn-out submarine scream, blood and air rushed from his blow hole, and foamed obscenely on the surface. He kicked twice, and then again, as he moved weakly away from the beach towards the open sea, leaving behind him a plume of blood like dark smoke hanging in the air; Orion's life-blood welling out into the ocean, leaving a streak like a scar on the face of the deep.

He managed to reach the surface, and made an agonised rasping noise that was a pitiful gasp for air, while the nausea swept through him. Air bubbled and foamed from both his blow hole and the wound. He kicked and bucked. Helpless in the confusion, the shock and the pain, he rolled in the disgustingly crimson sea all around him. He sank, spinning and twisting, choking and drowning in his own blood.

Sabre and his mother were half a mile off the beach when the bullet struck. They heard the thud of the impact followed by the terrifying scream. They both burst into a pulsing swim towards Orion, totally oblivious to any danger that must lie with him. They knew only that he was in terrible pain, that he needed them. By the time they reached Orion he was bumping on the sea-bed, enveloped in a large cloud of blood still billowing from the wound. The big bull was twice their size, but between them they lifted him towards the surface, turned him, and forced his back above the waves. He drew a hoarse weak breath and wallowed uselessly in the water, his great dorsal slapping the waves as it rolled drunkenly from side to side.

In his own state of shock the crofter stared at the scene unfolding before him. It was all outside his previous experience: some nightmare that just could not be real. He dropped the gun and it fell unnoticed on to the rocks. How could it happen? Deer and rabbits would bolt from their stricken comrades. Why should Grampus behave like this? How could a beast that killed like the whale act like this? Even as the first blood rose to the surface, and Orion screamed, the man saw the two shadows streaking towards the beach. Why didn't they go? Why must it be like this? The killer whale rolling helplessly out there, with his family struggling to keep him on the surface and push him to safety.

While the white-hot agony burnt along Orion's spine, Sabre and Nightshadow fought for his life, and the crofter willed him to die. But the big whale would not die yet. It would be several hours of energy-sapping agony before the wound took him: several hours while Orion swam his last pain-filled miles, fighting a battle that he could only lose. Hours, while Sabre and his frantic mother exhausted themselves for the dying whale.

Orion rolled over revealing a belly that was no longer white, but rose-tinted with his own blood. As he was rolled upright his bent dorsal swept above the surface, carrying water which sprayed in a vermilion fan into the waves.

The crofter swung around and stumbled off; unseeing; horrified; utterly shocked. The blanket fell from his shoulders. He never returned for his possessions, and they were carried away by the tide, the gun smashed by the waves against the weed-flecked stones.

Slowly the beach returned to normal. The seals settled, and the gulls began their scavenging day. Once again the falcon's shadow flicked, fork-winged, across the moor. Soon the animals of the island's shore had forgotten the shocking dawn, and to remind them there was only an ugly red stain running out to sea.

For the whales, however, the horror was far from over. Sabre and his mother pushed the bull slowly away from the beach towards the sanctuary and peace of deep water. Orion was helpless, and they knew that he would die. His once powerful flukes hung limp and useless. He had barely enough energy to breathe, and occasionally he sobbed a long weak moan from somewhere deep inside. And sometimes, when they nudged him a little too hard in their struggles to support him, the pain would shake his entire body, and he would scream, and the she-whale would cry to him.

Throughout the day his family kept Orion on the surface, pushing him gently to the west. He grew weaker by the hour, while his wound bled less freely. As the sun set in their path, the stricken whale took a last compulsive breath, gave a short cry of good-bye, and all agony drifted away with his life. They released him then, and watched the great whale, pink belly upwards, fall on his last journey to the sea floor. And when the darkness had swallowed him up they swam off into the dusk.

The red stain off Seal Island was gone by morning. With it had disappeared the fear the animals had known for the previous few days. For the seals there was no longer terror at the sight of the huge black fin cutting towards one of their comrades.

Repair

T HE KILLER WHALES, swimming fast and straight, had moved far out into the open Atlantic. First the sounds and smells of the coast-line had been left behind, and then the first big ocean rollers met them, and still they swam. Long after they felt the Shelf drop away beneath them they slowed down, and listened to the emptiness of the sea surrounding them. No sounds of fish, or seals, or porpoises. No crash of waves, or sizzle of surf. Even the wind was a mere whisper on the surface, and above all there was no sound from Orion, left far behind them on the bed of the Shelf.

For five days they drifted aimlessly, blowing infrequently and quietly. They were barely swimming, letting the tide carry them where it would. During this time they emitted no sonar noises, and the only sound they made was in their breathing. There was nothing to hear them or see them. They were completely alone. Aware only of the other's warm presence close by, they allowed their minds to sleep in silence, to bathe the shock from memory with the clean emptiness of the ocean.

The air grew very still, but colder, on the second day of their solitude, and soon a northern mist fell like a veil. The killer whales were cloaked in peace, and they adjusted willingly to the attitude of the weather. Relaxing, forgetting, sleeping, their whole awareness almost entirely shut down.

And so the North Atlantic allowed them to repair. When the mist cleared, and a light south-easterly lifted the seas into long sparkling rollers, there was still nothing to disturb them. From all points of the compass the ocean stretched away to infinity, meeting the sky on the distant horizon. The sky itself was occupied only by clouds, no birds travelling the empty sky-ways so far from land.

Sabre gradually awoke, reluctant at first to relinquish the shroud that enveloped him. He clicked, released long low notes, and listened for echoes. The sonar waves travelled far and deep. In the remote depths the waves met the barren sea floor and bounced back towards him, revealing that somewhere beneath him, in that chilling darkness, there was an end, a limit. Horizontally, through 360 degrees, distorted echoes returned. The whispers could have been anything, from shoals of fish, to the reefs of a lonely island, or possibly pockets of water of a different temperature from the surrounding seas. All was indeterminate and insubstantial. His vision told him no more; just bubbles in the clear water diffusing into the greyness.

Sabre, now a year old, was powerfully built, and almost as long as his mother's fourteen feet. He was no longer a calf and could fend for himself. With no effort he could keep up with Nightshadow on journeys of sustained high speed, though he was not yet capable of the fantastic bursts of acceleration which Orion had used during a hunt. With the approach of adolescence his hooked fin was just beginning to straighten and grow. One day it would be the enormous recurved weapon of an adult bull, and by that time he would have his father's great power.

Sabre had grown restless and impatient. When awake he repeatedly twisted around, snapping at shadows in the waves. Frustrated by mouthfuls of spray and foam, he frequently leapt into the air, and listened to the crashing and exploding in the swarm of bubbles as he reorientated himself.

His mother, now alert, and aware of his impatience, called him, and they moved together swimming slowly north-west, pausing beneath the smooth-faced rollers and spouting in the troughs.

They were still completely alone for there were no eyes to see their brief blows far beneath the heaving white-flecked crests; but company was fast approaching from the north. Forty bottle-nosed dolphins sped across the surface, leaping gracefully over the deep valleys and riding down the waves. Long effervescent wakes of white water marked their swift passage, and they emitted chirping and whistling noises to one another as they hurtled into the air. All sleek, streamlined individuals, they broke the surface as one body. Well fed and careless after a summer in the cool waters of the sub-arctic, the school, mainly cows and calves, now raced ahead of the winter like fat silver-grey arrows across the sea. The boars flanked and led the school. Up to twelve feet in length, they guarded the happy dolphins, and listened to the hissing ocean as it rushed by.

They appeared suddenly on the edge of Sabre's sonar. He clicked once, and heard only fuzzy infinity, the hush of mile upon mile of pitching water. He clicked again, and there they were: a mass of humping echoes hurrying towards him. At once he accelerated, calling for his mother to follow. She swam behind him, half-heartedly at first, but as the high-pitched plopping and whistling

51

drew nearer she pushed on harder, and by the time they reached the dolphins she was at Sabre's side, galloping amongst the panic, snapping with her deadly jaws, and kicking with her flukes at the grey targets as they twisted away.

A head-on collision with a boar dolphin stunned Sabre for a few precious moments. A flicker of grey brought him back to his senses, and with angry determination he sped after the boar, singling him out for the kill, ignoring the other grey flashes shooting by. He snapped at the dolphin's tail, but missed by a foot, and felt the sweep of water blast into his face. Now, furious, he hurled himself forward. The hunter and the hunted raced, bullet straight, across the face of the deep; muscles tearing, lungs screaming, and hearts thudding to meet the demands of the chase. The dolphin swam for his life, but began to slow as he gasped in the cool air. He felt Sabre in thunderous pursuit behind him, and tried a desperate turn to the left, but this time the whale's jaws closed over the desperate beast's abdomen. There was an explosive shock of battle, and then the dolphin lay torn in ugly death.

Presently Sabre was joined by his mother, and together they wolfed down the hot flesh, satisfying their hunger, until they found themselves awash once more on a silent sea.

The Great School

NIGHTSHADOW WAS SLOWER to recover than Sabre. Orion's death left a vacuum in her being. Over the years she had grown too dependent on the big bull. He had guided her, and hunted for her; he had listened for sounds of danger rippling through the sea, and guarded her from any challenger. Now, in his absence, she grew lonely, the proximity of Sabre being the only reminder of the life she had learnt to expect.

Sabre took over the role of hunter, and with his mother's help, he scratched a living from the autumn ocean. Without Orion's keen senses to rely upon, his sonar became sharper. He learnt to hear the dolphins before they located him. He discovered that he could close the distance between himself and his prey by hiding on the sea floor, or by swimming along a wave until the moment of the strike: but, like his mother, he was lonely. There was an emptiness about their existence: the spark of life had dulled. Sabre was fleet of fin, swift to kill, and alert to many more sounds and vibrational murmurs that moved upon the tide than he had ever noticed while Orion had led them, but when clothed with the softness of night, he and his mother listened to the whispering sea and remembered different days.

On the October gales the two killer whales rode towards the Faroe Isles. Fate had brought them to this remote corner of the world, mid-way between the Shetlands and Iceland. Not for the fish they found in the island voes, or for the Pilot whale they found dying near the rocks; but, as winter's curtain fell, they found friends.

Flippers quivering in surprise, Sabre awoke to a sound from the past. It was no louder than the wind whining in the crests, or the current surging over the rocks beneath him, yet it woke him, and set his quick brain working. He sank deeper, and listened. His mother fell towards him; she too had been rocked into alertness by the brief sound. It came again, stronger and closer. Sabre had heard it so often before, had made the same noises himself, and as more and more of the high-pitched notes pinged in his ears, he accelerated towards them, for they were the calls of killer whales.

Black and white bodies danced about them wherever they looked, and the sea was full of the happy voices of whales. Cows, calves, and adolescents everywhere. In the lambent first light of day, a glowing phosphorescent wake followed each whale as it sped, in tight circles, round the newcomers. Sabre and Nightshadow basked at the centre of attention, watching the flowing after-glow encircling them, and the ring of whales, with their clicking chirping song.

The whale dance slowed and stopped. On the outskirts of his vision, Sabre caught glimpses of a grey form, circling, ghost-like and immense, prowling silently at the boundaries of the pod. A corridor formed between the whales, and the grey shape darkened and grew as it swam towards them. The shape materialised into an enormous bull killer whale. Grossly scarred, and with a harpoon-torn dorsal, the bull was master of the Great School. His name was Forkfin. In the sudden silence Sabre became afraid, as Forkfin loomed huge above

54

them. With his instinctive, careless bravery Sabre
growled, and moved threateningly between his mother
and the bull. A colossal sweep of water pushed him aside,
and a strange calm fell. They hung there, Sabre and
Nightshadow, dwarfed beneath the steady stare of the
Master.

Sabre was not too old to be accepted by the big bull,
and the she-whale had not screamed out for a protector.
Behind the ugly grey skull the decision was made.
Forkfin accepted the two whales into the Great School.
They were no longer alone.

The old leader called, soft voiced, and the killers
moved off. In untidy array, towards the south, long
processions of fins hooked in the spray. In front of them
all, the tall riven fin rode imperiously above the swell,
and pointed the destiny of the pod.

Forkfin was a whale of the high Arctic. Born beneath
the towering white heights of icebergs, he quickly learnt
how to survive amongst the frozen wastes. While still a
calf, barely weaned, his family had been caught against
the solid wall of a berg, as a surge of ice swept over them.
Forkfin was the only survivor. For cruel months Death
hung about him. The Arctic ocean fed him, while his
character was hewn from the frozen environment.

It was as a powerful, ruthless adult, that Forkfin eventually left the ice-fields, and ploughed his way into the
southern seas. Beneath the permanent summer sun of
Norway's North Cape, he gathered his first pod. For
years, happy and secure in the abundant seas, he led his
ever growing family between Iceland and Norway,
until, one terrible day, the whalers followed him into a
fjord. He lost them all, the entire pod, harpooned against
the sheer glacier-carved walls. Two harpoons hit him,

one gouging along his flank, and the other smashing his
dorsal; but the whalers could not catch him. For the
second time in his life he found himself alone on a hostile
sea. He turned away from Norway's coast, leaving the
steep-walled fjords and the blue-veined ice-mantles
behind him for ever.

This time he remained a loner for many years, while he
learnt the ways of the temperate seas. Ever since that day
when the waters of the fjord ran red with the blood of his
cows and calves, he felt insecure close to land. He therefore spent most of his chosen isolation in the blue water.
Out there, beyond the shelf, with the empty acres
beneath him, he began to grow old.

Now, many years later, he was master of the Great
School. Even when the oldest cows had been gathered,
or taken by force from the mastery of lesser bulls, he was
no longer young, and many scar-filled years had drifted
by since then. The pod flourished under his unfailing
command. Sometimes his wards did not understand, but
they always obeyed. The far off buzz of high-speed
propellers was enough for him to steer the whole pod out
into the silent ocean. As sole escort to his convey he met
his responsibilities unerringly, so that, against all odds,
few members of the Great School were lost.

Sabre was leaner than most of the adolescents of his
age, though he was longer, and stronger. He had never
had the playful company of calves before, and now he
made up for lost time. Riding the green rollers they
chased about, nipping each other's tails. They surged on
long, white-capped breakers, and sang with the cows
after a hunt. On moonlit nights, while the school slept
and cast shadows into the deep, Sabre swam among the
moon-swords, dodging or rushing through them, snap-

ping and sporting. Usually he was unaware of Forkfin's observation, as the great giant swam, unseen, around the perimeter of the school. Sabre knew nothing of the fire that shone behind Forkfin's eyes. Memories of the past, of his own early youth, before the ice deaths, flashed through the old bull's mind while he watched the care-free adolescent. Amongst the young bulls Sabre alone was unafraid of the great whale, and often, night or day, Forkfin's attention would be held by this one barely a third his size.

On the surface of a winter ocean the dark backs of the Great School slid and breached. Their blows were whisked away on the cool northern breeze, and the white patterns upon their heads and flanks merged with the lines of foam. Often noisy, almost confused and careless in their motion, then swift, barely seen shadows in the curl of a wave, they moved landward, where in the impending spring, the seals and the salmon would col-lect; though even in the shallows, with the sound of waves booming on to rocks and cliffs loud in their ears, they still found the surface grey and empty. Forkfin sent hunting groups to the floor to search out cod shoals, but there were few to find.

On a cold day at the end of March, a cow, patrolling the sea-bed, discovered a wreck. She called to the school above her, and Forkfin brought them to a halt. Then, in pairs, the killers descended into the purple twilight to hunt around. The invaders from the surface found cod and pouting darting through the smashed metal rigging; and deeper, beneath the overhanging keel, golden pol-lock met their end as they fled into the inky shadows. Ling, sleek and long, bearded with a single sensitive barbule, stole about close to the sea-bed, but they too were found by the repeating sonar. Dark conger eels writhed from port-holes, tempted into the open by the bitter smell of blood beginning to hang over the wreck.

Once the wreck had been a warship, cruising the North Atlantic, helping to protect the world from Hitler's war-machine. One moonless night, on Christmas Eve, a U-boat had found her, and sent a torpedo to tear out her guts. Now she lay there, tide-worn, the home of creatures of the ocean floor. Where the torpedo had struck was a vast hole, and inside was an impenetrable darkness, sinister and foreboding. Deep in the hole, where men had once eaten, and celebrated Christmas, and dreamt of the end of the war, before the exploding charge had blasted their hopes away, lived the biggest conger of the wreck. Jet black, with tiny eyes, he rarely ventured from his lair. He skulked in the darkness waiting for his prey, anything that swam or crawled unsuspectingly into the metal pit, where his gaping jaws closed swiftly and finally.

Life teemed about the wreck. As soon as the stench of oil and war had left her the corals and shell-fish had moved in, changing her, wrapping her in a calcerous blanket, softening her harsh metal outline. Crabs and lobsters invaded the sea floor around her, and octopuses climbed upon her decks. Fish and squid found sanctuary and abounding food, and soon a large community made a home in the old hulk. In summer a halo of silver-green mackerel sparkled about her, and ghostly grey tope stole down from the surface to hunt in her rigging.

The master of the wreck, the huge conger, was attacked by nothing: not even the sharks that visited the wreck briefly in the warmer months dared enter his hole.

Now, for the first time in his long life, killer whales

had arrived, and the wreck-serpent, safe in the darkness, listened to the clicks and hunting cries of the new enemy, and smelt the blood seeping farther into the depths of the wreck.

Eventually the sounds and smells of violent death enticed him into action. He slid towards the entrance, writhed over the edge, and swam down, towards the bottom. At first he was protected from the probing sonar by clouds of silver scales. Above him he caught glimpses of white-bellied whales, and when he reached the bed he saw fish carcasses being torn apart by crabs and lobsters. He gulped down all he found, unmoved by clawing lobsters attacking his tough hide.

He prowled beneath the wreck for a long time, hidden in the poor light. Then the quick eyes of a young cow found his huge form slithering across the purple rocks. The conger sensed the whale's approach, and coiling himself, like an immense python, he reared his great head. The gash of his mouth yawned open as he prepared to strike. As the cow closed in the conger swayed his head gently, like kelp waving in the tide; a hypnotic, seductive movement. The whale hesitated, sensing something dangerous about the eel; but with the sounds of her comrades striking around her, she opened her mouth, while her flukes nudged her forward.

Dimly she was aware of an aching throb in her mouth. She had seen no movement, but as the shock wore off she felt a white-hot pain. She loosed a cloud of bubbles as she screamed and wrenched herself free, leaving a segment of her tongue in the conger's jaws. She bolted for the surface, leaving a gallon of dark blood billowing in her wake. Silence fell on the sea, as the Great School stopped their hunt and swam to her aid.

59

Forkfin curved towards the whimpering cow. As the blood gushed from her mouth she grew dizzy, and partly from shock, and partly from loss of blood, she lost consciousness, while the big grey whale stared at her.

He dropped away, leaving the elder cows to tend the injured huntress. He followed her pluming trail to the sea floor. On the surface the blood-leached sea was livid red, but as he descended the colour became blue, and on the bed itself it hung in a black cloud, wafting in the tide.

Forkfin settled on to the rocks, his frozen gaze piercing into the shadows. He waited for the monster out there to betray itself. Presently one of the shadows moved. Forkfin inched himself over the floor towards the swaying serpent. He saw the thick girth of the eel, and the gaping, ready mouth.

There was a flash in the darkness and a mushroom of sand. Close by were thumping, scraping noises. In the instant before the old whale could lunge, Sabre had curled around him, and head-crashed into the eel.

The quick-ferocious noise of the fight died. Forkfin, suddenly anxious in the quiet, called out. As the sand settled, there before the master's glowering gaze was Sabre, with the eel hanging lifeless from his mouth. There was no call of praise from the old whale, but on their journey to the surface, with Sabre dragging his proud kill, a fire burnt behind Forkfin's eyes. In the ways of whales the old master was impressed, and Forkfin had not been impressed for many years.

For two cold weeks Forkfin carried the injured cow, as she drifted between twitching sleep, and the agony of consciousness. He held her at the surface so that she could breathe, even when the gales tried to wash his burden away. He sent her sisters to hunt for her. With a soft, private voice, he soothed the she-whale through her aching nights, until her fever passed, and the swollen tongue repaired itself. When she began to support herself at the surface he left her, knowing that she would survive, guided by her halo of anxious cows.

The wreck soon found another master; a conger eel, writhing in the man-made holds. The fish returned, and the bodies disappeared beneath the claws of the crabs.

Where Orion had been forced to stop, Forkfin and the Great School took over. Even had he lived, Orion could never have taught Sabre in the way of a killer whale pack, for long ago a whaler's shadow had spread across his pod. Only he and Nightshadow had escaped the gun. Together they could teach Sabre to hunt, but not in the ways of a pack.

Mostly there was the barest thread of discipline and order in the pod, but Forkfin could snap them into an organised pack of sea-wolves with one sharp call whenever he needed them.

In the hungry times Forkfin spaced out his killers so that a long bow stretched across miles of ocean. In this way their sonar range was increased, and with a zig-zag course, they covered, with tremendously lethal effect, a far larger area than a group travelling at random could have achieved. When they found no food the Master formed them into an arrow-head formation; each whale swimming in the slipstream of the one in front. For many days they could swim like this, saving energy, at sustained high speed, until a new prey fell across their path, or a storm broke above them.

Guided by the secrets in his old mind and the sounds of food, or just where he sensed it was safe, Forkfin led his killer convoy.

The Great School swam south. They cruised through the North Channel which divides Ireland from southern Scotland, and into the Irish Sea, rocked by tumbling, gale-lashed March seas. They found little prey here, but much noise. Sleek NATO destroyers thrust a creaming wake through the waves; ferry boats churned ponderously back and forth, and deep-sea trawlers returned gratefully from their perilous visits to the open North Atlantic fishing grounds. This was a sea concentrated with ships. For centuries men had fished and fought upon these waters, and their noise had increased through the ages. Protected from the Atlantic's bulk by the islands of Britain, whales often sought sanctuary and food here, only to find themselves out-numbered by man's malignant presence.

Forkfin grew anxious, and pushed the Great School on through the crowded seas. Sandy shores met them, and in the distance, shrouded in mists of rain, were the hills of North Wales, not yet bursting with the green of spring. Still the hunting was poor, with just a few seals and sparse fish shoals to support them. The whales grew lean and quick tempered, the young bulls fighting each other with a spark of fire in their battles: bared teeth, flukes sweeping with malice and forethought towards their targets ... Hints of male adulthood seeping into their swim, accentuated by hunger. Forkfin countenanced the fights, but stopped them before serious injury could occur. Usually a sharp call was enough: if not a heavy thud in the flank from the Master's grey head never failed to dull a young bull's anger.

Sabre had one enemy in the Great School: a big rogue bull called Red-Eye. A year older than Sabre, Red-Eye was fast approaching the time of his exile. Forkfin, like any other dominant leader of a killer whale pack, could not tolerate any other mature bull. Red-Eye was very nearly an adult. The rogue had chosen Sabre as his main target amongst the young bulls. Possibly Red-Eye sensed something of the strange bond that was forming between Sabre and Forkfin, and in attacking Sabre was challenging Forkfin's command. The conflicts were never dangerous, the grey Master saw to that, but they were traumatic in their spray-laden speed. So Sabre learnt, at an early age, how to defend himself.

They left the coast of West Wales behind them, and still they swept on, killing, away from the Pembroke coast, feeling the warm push of the Atlantic in their faces. Three days later they crossed the Bristol Channel and were off the storm beaches of North Cornwall. Here, at least, spring had come, and while the primroses opened in the Cornish meadows and brightened the banks of roads and rivers, the salmon arrived in the estuaries. Life, here, was beginning to stir. In the long lines of white surf marching up the gently shelving beaches, bass hunted for sand-eels: these silver wolves of the coast rode in with the waves, sometimes in no more than six inches of water. They swam swiftly over the sand, watching for the tell-tale puff of yellow that betrayed a sand-eel scurrying into the shallows. Big black cormorants sat on the rocks, gazing, with bored expressions, at the heaving seas. They marked their territories, preened, and prepared to raise their young, and anticipated the eagerly awaited mackerel promised by the warmer weather.

Fat herring gulls floated, sharp-eyed, just beyond the beach rollers, or flew, searching the waters for early shoals. With the gannets they dropped on closed wings, head first, into the sea, throwing up thin white spouts. All they found were plaice on the sandy bed, or small shoal bass. But the mackerel were coming.

Even along these awakening shores there was not enough food for so many killer whales, and the fishing boats dotted around the coast constantly alerted Forkfin.

They left as swiftly and as deadly as they had arrived. The cormorants and the shags watched them go: many fins, and many backs, breaking the surface of the sea as one curving body, and ahead of them all a mighty riven fin: the leader. Their spout, a thick repeating shock of noise, drowned, for brief seconds, the sound of the surf, and then they were gone.

The seas of Cornwall, Wolf Rock and the Scilly Isles were to be the killers' last taste of British shores for over a year. Forkfin was leading them on a journey that would end only at the sun-baked sands of North Africa.

At first they headed due west, until they were beyond the shelf. Here, on the open ocean, a few nomadic seals or a shoal of porpoises were their only company. The occasional propellers to disturb Forkfin were those of giant oil tankers, slowly pushing their laden bulk towards hungry dependants in Britain and Europe. Then the School turned due south, with the westerly currents and winds washing green seas over their backs.

For the sake of the calves the Great School moved slowly now, and Forkfin sent small hunting groups away from the main pod to search out prey in the undisturbed seas. He dived on his own into the ocean deep, and returned with cuttle-fish and squid for his hungry wards.

They roamed across the wide heaving surface of the Bay of Biscay, until at the end of May they found themselves becalmed off a peaceful coast. Behind them and to the west lay Biscay and the North Atlantic. To their south and east the yellow-brown mountains of Spain climbed above the horizon, and waved, drunkenly, in the heat haze.

Forkfin led his pod quietly through these heady seas, keeping them just out of sight of questing eyes along the cliffs of the Spanish coast. The sea was murky with blooms of plankton, and noisy with the harvesting of plankton feeders. Sardine shoals swarmed in the abundance like herring in northern seas. These tiny fish fell in turn to the mackerel and shoals of tuna, huge cousins of the mackerel. Amongst these came the porpoises, dolphins and seals, crazy and carefree in the warm bloom. The sharks were there; somewhere: circling torpedo shapes, snarling makos and porbeagles, shoals of small blues and lone threshers, striking dark blurs appearing, evil-faced, on the edge of the harvest.

Plankton carpeted the sea and supported a glut of predators. As in any other year the transient excess would soon fade, but in the meantime the Great School shared in the richness created by the bloom, as they made their way along the coast.

The rocky shores of Spain were no longer a land-mark for the killer whales. Once again countless acres of empty sea-water lay beneath them, terminating two miles down on the floor. Again they pushed on, following the invisible migration lanes of the humpback whales down the eastern fringes of the Atlantic. They saw no humpbacks, though occasionally, at the limits of hearing, they heard these great baleen whales. The humpbacks, 'singing whales', were several hundred miles to the north of the Great School, drifting in the warm push of the Gulf Stream. The singing whales called to very few ears, for every year the 'pirate' whalers found their migration lanes, and intercepted the fragmented groups. The humpbacks that the Great School heard were mere dwindling relics of a species that had once crowded the sea-lanes from the equator, up past the coast of West Africa, and all the way to the northern British Isles. Now Forkfin's pod failed to meet a single one of these whales that could have meant full stomachs for every killer whale in the pack for over a week. Sabre, in the stillness of the night, listened to their song through the billions of cubic miles of ocean that separated the killers from the humpbacks. They never drew any nearer: perhaps violent history, and the wisdom of heredity, had taught the singing whales to stay clear of an enemy that was almost as deadly as the whalers.

The north east trades replaced the westerlies and the whales made good progress. Even while they slept at night the following seas carried them south. Now they did little hunting, for they were entering tropical seas, and they had no need to build up thick layers of insulating blubber. Instead they fed on prey that fell across their path, and grew lethargic and slow under the oppressive heat of the sun.

On a blazing July day they arrived. The burnt smell of Africa drifted out over the waves. The Great School was in one of the hottest regions of the earth. Away to their east lay the Atlas mountains, and beyond that barren range lay the Sahara desert, the sun's anvil. With air temperatures of over a hundred degrees Fahrenheit, the only relief for the killer whales was the relatively cool

Canaries current, seeping gently from the north. The sun beat down from white skies all through the long days, scorching the land, and evaporating millions of tons of water from the sea. Land plants wilted and died. The ocean slept, beaten into temporary submission by the intense heat.

Farther to the south, between the Tropic of Cancer and the equator, Africa was being drenched by monsoon rains, but the north west continent was suffering the peak of the dry season. The land cracked and disfigured under the white heat, the waves lapped weakly upon the yellow sands, and steam rose from the shore-side rocks. Animals hiding in the shade waited for the merciful cool of the night.

The killer whales wallowed languidly at the surface, also waiting for the relief of evening. Almost as a physical shock sunset fell. One moment there was the beating searing heat, and then the sun was red and sinking into the Atlantic's horizon. Then it was gone, and the stars flicked into the night sky. The moon and the star-glow lit a different world. As soon as the sun dropped out of sight tiny pockets of movement scurried over the sand. The killer whales lay just off a gently sloping beach. From this beach to the other side of the Sahara desert, almost three thousand miles distant, the story was the same, with only minor variations. From burrows that were virtually invisible by day, Kangaroo rats poked their whiskers out into the lunar light. Spiders, some huge some tiny, climbed upon the dunes. Lizards scampered after insects, their quick-moving feet noisy in the desert silence. Snakes, totally hidden by day beneath rock and sand, slithered about their business, venom ready and fast. Owls and falcons, small by comparison with their northern cousins, stole across the star-scape, their shadows moving swiftly over the desert terrain.

The sea was lit in its own special way. Every wave was tipped with the glow of phosphorescent plankton, and even the sandy bed shone through the tropical night. Here, as on the land, the hunters awoke, and life became brisk and purposeful. Unlike the land the sea held its warmth, so that by dawn the temperature was little less than that at dusk. Away from the sea, all across the desert the temperature fell rapidly, the heat escaping from the sand into the clear skies, so that by sunrise it was well below zero.

A camel coughed somewhere in the sand-dunes, the sun glowed fiercely in the east and the stars vanished. The night's survivors hurried into the shade as the new desert day flushed, orange, across North Africa.

The Great School basked, without a care, at the surface. Forkfin was troubled only by a few sail-powered dhows out fishing. The whales fed on sun-fish and tuna. The former were vast, sometimes over a ton in weight, and very easy to catch. The killers swam amongst coral reefs, and scratched themselves along the calcerous under-sea cities, removing parasites clinging to their hides. In this multi-coloured, sky-swept sea they spent the entire summer, growing, playing and hunting: a reprieve from the real ocean they had left behind in the north.

The sea was not totally without its dangers. Sharks increasingly bothered the Great School. Mainly blues and makos, the sharks' targets were the whale calves that played unsuspectingly at the fringe of the pod. Out of the murky waters the snarling faces would appear, twisting towards the calves. Usually the attacks were futile, and

ended in the death of a shark; the calves would bolt, and
several cow whales would speed in towards the mean-
eyed assailants. Killer whales swim faster than sharks. A
thud in the side from a whale moving at thirty miles an
hour could kill or stun a shark. Then within minutes the
hapless fish would be torn to pieces, and devoured by its
frenzied comrades, until only a cloud of blood in the sea
marked the shark's folly. Sometimes a calf would be
injured by a shark before the cows became aware of the
attack, and this could be very dangerous for the School.
Blood attracted quick-finned hunters from many miles
away, and on one of these occasions an injured calf drew
the menacing attention of a Great White shark.

A Hammerhead was responsible for the initial damage. While the calf was being harassed by a shoal of blues,
the hammerhead rushed in, unseen, from beneath, and
ripped away half of one of the calf's fore-flippers. Before
it had swum thirty yards the shark was dead, its chest
torn open by the injured whale's mother.

While blood oozed from the calf's flipper the sharks
became increasingly agitated, and more and more
appeared, until they far out-numbered the Great School.
The hammerhead was devoured, and then the sharks
turned their attention on the whale calf.

Suddenly every adult member of the Great School was
required to protect the calves. There were sharks everywhere: too many. The jaws of a swift mako caught the
skin of a cow before her tail could accelerate her away
from danger. Beneath the tropical sun a battle was being
fought that was to last all day: killer whales with their
calculating mammalian brains, superior speed and
protective instincts, versus opponents with insignificant
minds but an acute sense of smell, and a suicidal purpose.

Forkfin killed few of the sharks. He held himself back, constantly using his sonar, saving his strength for the real danger he knew swam somewhere out there in the distance.

The Great White was a monster: longer than Forkfin and about the same weight, the shark knew all about killing. It had swum the warm seas for years, destroying anything in its path. It had eaten its brethren, and all manner of fish from the deep and the surface. It had even eaten men; fishermen, taken from boats too small to withstand the Great White's attack. Many times it had tasted the flesh of whales. In its cavernous stomach lay evidence of the shark's voracity. There were tin cans, chunks of wood, the wheel of a car, rocks, a propeller ... all kinds of junk collected over years of ocean wanderings.

The huge fish heard the sounds of violence in the sea, and the bitter taste of blood drew it inexorably towards the Great School. Tragically, Forkfin was on the wrong side of the pod when the shark attacked. A massive grey blur, jaws agape, swept above the injured calf. One bite removed the stricken whale's tail, and the grey shape sped off into the gloom, turning, preparing for another attack. Sabre, Red-Eye and three cow whales rushed in pursuit of the Great White. If they had caught it they might have been destroyed, for the shark was too large, and its jaws possessed a power that could break them in two. Their own teeth would have had little effect on the armoured hide.

Forkfin blasted them all aside, his roar quenching the sounds of battle elsewhere. This shark belonged to him. He had met the colossal beasts before, and it was his calf that lay back there, tailless, its life almost over.

Sabre watched as the two grey shapes merged into one. A swollen mushroom of billowing water, thirty yards across, formed at the surface, as Forkfin crashed into the shark's belly. The two great bodies locked together and twisted down into the sea, their tails slapping and thrashing as they fell. Then, as they became lost in the deep, there was silence, and the other sharks were gone. Forkfin reappeared, and swam back, alone and victorious, to his School. A red gash ran down the length of his flank, and a single triangular tooth, six inches across at its base, lay embedded in his head. At this moment the Great White was being torn to pieces by the other sharks, and such a carcass would take even these blood-crazed scavengers time enough for the killer whales to steal away into the ocean.

The tailless calf whimpered out of her coma. In one deliberate movement Forkfin took her into his mouth and she lay dead, her skull crushed by her father's jaws. He carried her, far out into the deep water, the Great School forming two walls on either side of the Master and his burden. He released her then, and they watched her fall away, rolling over on the slow Canaries tide. Her mother swam down into the sea with her, but returned to Forkfin's soft calls when the darkness had swallowed her calf.

Slowly the Great School swam up the west coast of Africa. It was now January, and Forkfin was leading them back to the north, where they would arrive by early spring. It was the coolest time of year for this coast of the continent, though most days the temperatures rose into the eighties and beyond. Rain came, briefly, though hardly enough to ruffle the dusty surface of the desert. Here and there a patch of green made a tentative appearance, before the blistering heat, and the attentions of thirsty animals, reduced it to crumbling brown fragments blowing across the dunes.

The sea was caught in a confusion of currents and winds. The cool Canaries' drift washed into their faces together with steep seas, lifted by brisk north-east trades, laden with sand and dust from the desert. Moist south-west maritime trades followed the whales, shortening the distance between the crests, and cooling the air.

So the Great School left Africa. To Sabre it had been another set of lessons, more learning crammed into his alert mind: coral ablaze with colour and light, sun-dappled sands, sharks and sun-fish, friends and good hunting, a searing dryness in the air: that, to Sabre and the Great School, was the African coast. He knew nothing, consciously, of the importance of the massive continent, though undoubtedly messages from eons past lay locked in his genes. For Africa was the birthplace of so many species. Even human-kind began here, treading, carefully, out over the lush savannah, an aggressive intelligence welling behind dark eyes. Long before this, before the pre-men were born of the apes, species of cetacea, the whales, crowded upon sun-swept beaches. They swam out to sea, and learnt how to survive in an ocean glowering with menace. This, and all that had evolved since, lay instinctively within Sabre's mind and body, and guided him and his kind into the future, towards an unknown destiny, and an unknown purpose.

Three winters and two summers after Sabre had joined the Great School, the time came for him to leave. They had been cold wild winters, cruel winters, the pod surviving, with few casualties, only because of Forkfin's leadership. In the summers they flourished, and the calves played, their bodies curling over the sun-sparkled surface. In the autumn the pod grew. The heavy, swollen cows lagged behind, until something made Forkfin halt the School in a quiet corner of the ocean. Here the quickening pulse of life within them forced the cows to thrash their flukes, or hang limply at the surface. Tail first, usually at dawn, the calves were born, and for the next few days they gulped the last of the summer air, or nestled beneath their mother's flippers, staring, baffled, into their tilting world.

After the cold months, when a new warmth drifted from the shallows, the hormones flooded fire through the bodies of the males. Forkfin's patience ebbed, and some luckless bull, calling in rage once too often, fell under the Master's frozen stare.

Sabre was now too old, and his dorsal too long. His back was too broad, and desire ate at his belly. His play with the cows became something more than a game, and in the stillness of night he bellowed, and grew aggressive. At first Forkfin seemed not to notice, but in the end, in the first light of an April day, Sabre awoke to the sight of the scarred grey head.

The new hormones drove resentment and bitterness into Sabre's brain, so that later he could not recall the head crashing, or the snarling, and the thrusting driving flukes, and the churning white foam. Forkfin met all Sabre's attacks, and gave back just slightly more; but unlike the younger whale he knew exactly what he was doing. His was not the bitter battle invoked by male restlessness, but the calculating, almost kind, strategy of the old and wise. At last Sabre turned away, and swam off into the jade green distance.

Whale

His mother and Forkfin watched his going. Together with the Great School they clicked and chirped, and sang their farewells, and listened in his wake long after the distance and the waves had swallowed his echo. Perhaps they would soon forget that they had once loved a young bull whale called Sabre; or perhaps ... ?

Alone

FOR THE FIRST time in his life Sabre was completely alone. Several times he had wanted to turn back, to find the Great School and swim again with the calves, and dive with the old Master; but then the fires flared in his belly. He curved over the pitching crests, and fell head-long down the cascades, smooth as oil, into the enveloping valleys between the waves. He called out, expecting the ready answers from his friends, but there was only the welling water, and the harsh colours in the freshness of early spring. No turning back was possible.

Being fat and powerful he had no immediate need to hunt. Inside he felt only a faint urge to continue his course towards the north, for somewhere up there, beneath the bright star, something reached for him.

The Norwegian sea met him, cold and steep. Long swells rode powerfully along his back, and turned up, ridged and white capped, above the thrust of his tail. His body began to ache under the constant stress of his journey. Few sounds came to cheer him, and only the occasional surprise gave him any interest amongst the relentless currents pushing south.

Two Sperm whales provided him brief moments of terror. Both bulls, one very young, the other huge and angry, materialised from the grey at Sabre's flank. Red eyes, glowing with menace, stared from the enormous ugly heads at the lone killer whale, as he was held in the suction of a building wave.

With a roar, the incredibly long lower jaw of the older bull fell away from the blunt-nosed skull. Sabre caught a fleeting glimpse of the rows of chipped yellow teeth, as his tail launched him through the closing jaws. There was a clashing of enamel, and for an instant of horror, Sabre found himself caught, by the tip of his flukes, in the jaws of the great beast. He felt himself being dragged backwards with awesome power, and saw the jaws of the younger whale part and turn towards him. With a panicked burst of power he tore himself free, and crash-dived away from his assailants. He heard their great bulk hurtling after him into the gloom. The sperm whales bellowed their fury after him until they lost his twisting echo amongst the rustle of the waves.

Sabre felt even more alone. He had found enemies in these alien waters so far to the north. Beneath him were the impenetrable deeps; behind him, in the warmer seas of the Scottish Isles, lay all he knew. Before him was the frightening unknown, an unfeeling void. And yet somehow, something pulled at him from far beyond the blue line of the horizon.

Except for the occasional cloud of krill, Sabre found little food at the surface. His hunger roused his curiosity of the extreme deep. Forkfin had often dived with Sabre into the sub-deep, down to pitch-dark reefs on the edge of the Continental Shelf; but the old Master had never taken him down into the colossal darkness of the Atlantic beyond the Shelf.

Under the protest of his gurgling stomach the young bull shot a high spout into the air, turned over a crest, and head-dived down the steep wall of a wave. Instead of turning up beneath the trough he plunged on towards the ocean bed.

Quickly he descended, driven by slow sweeps of his tail, into the purpling emptiness of the mid-deep. Darkness swallowed him, and a peaceful cloak of silence banished the noise of the waves above. He fell, almost vertically, into the velvet quiet of the extreme deep. There his sonar picked up the sound of the floor, rushing to meet him. With each few fathoms, an extra ton of pressure wrapped around him; but his body was designed for such hostile effects. His rib-cage collapsed quietly as he thrust deeper. His lungs hurt, and his sonar rang gently in his ears; but these phenomena wore off as he grew accustomed to the heaviness of the abyss.

Sabre settled on to silt-covered rock. Two miles of water lay between him and the light. Wrapped in the warm darkness, unhindered by the wisp of any current, he began to cruise, sometimes hovering and echo-locating above the slit. He was about to turn for the surface when he saw a light. Moving across his line of vision a faint luminescence grew and faded. Then, in the shallow crevice of a rock, he saw another, brighter than the first, and quite motionless. He stopped and stared into the eerie light. Presently he became aware of a hideous face, cracked by an enormous gaping mouth lined with dark jagged teeth. The creature was an angler fish. The light source that had attracted Sabre was the fish's bait, produced by a specialised group of cells at the tip of a rod-like projection from the angler's head. As the whale watched, a tiny semi-transparent fish approached the dangling light. In an explosion of silt the angler's jaws closed upon its victim. The light went out.

On the fissured ocean floor death was swift and brutal, and the animals had adapted varied methods to kill and to survive. Most of the creatures were doomed to living out their entire lives in the awesome environment of the extreme deep. A few migrated, daily, up into the middle reaches of the sea, perhaps to catch a brief glimpse of the light, and to hunt in these less restricting depths. A few, like Sabre and the sperm whales, were mere visitors, tolerating, for a very short while, the acuteness of high pressure in an environment almost as hostile as the vacuum of space.

This inner space, where ugly life and sudden death were all there was, all there could be, became Sabre's hunting ground as he beat on into the northern ocean. Squid were his prey. Sometimes he found none, and often he found them in shoals, fanning their way across the gloom. He caught them as they fled into the darkness to hide from him, squirting ink in his face to throw him off their trail, and once, after a long high-pressure descent, he met an exceptionally large specimen. The killer whale settled on to the ocean bed. There was a dense haze of silt which muffled his sonar. No lights showed, and the creatures of the ocean floor seemed to be sleeping away some of the permanent night of their silent world. He moved off, echo-locating casually, cruising across the contours of the undulating terrain. He neither heard nor saw any sound or movement, and yet he sensed something malevolent. The whale was frightened by the blackness and silence of the rocks that surrounded him, or by something that hid amongst those rocks. He stopped and listened, his senses probing out into the darkness.

The giant squid reached towards the killer whale. Long tentacles snaked delicately around Sabre's body, deceitful in their soft touch. Before he could kick clear

Alone

the squid held him in a strangle-hold. A massive strength dragged him relentlessly, and he found himself being pulled into the rocks. His flukes drove in vain, and soon they too were trapped in the net of tentacles. He felt himself roll. Already exposed here to the uniform weight of a mile depth of water, he felt the crushing uneven force of the squid's hug. The pain became stifling and his heart thudded, while his brain clouded with the horror of helpless claustrophobia. With a burst of strength derived from his desperation, he managed to turn and attack, furiously, the squid's mantle. He struggled for a long time, using up his precious air, before the tentacles released him. Dazed, he shot clear, and ran head first into a wall of rock. All sense vanished in the total darkness. He was disorientated and parts of his body stung. His heart thumped in his ears, and he felt himself suffocating.

The agony of his long ascent seemed to last for ever. A tightness clamped down over his head as, starved of oxygen, he rushed on through the dark, feeling the pressure slowly, painfully, fall away, and a burning sensation begin to sear through his muscles.

He did not remember seeing the gloom of the sub-deep, nor the approaching whiteness of the surface. With his heart pounding in his chest the noise of the waves was deadened. But there was the incredible cool sweetness of the northern air while he blew continuously, throwing up high gusts of vapour into the sky.

Now the realisation that the sea was full of enemies was vivid and tangible. He had not learnt everything in the Great School. There were sperm whales on the surface, while in the deep there was the treacherous darkness, the deceitful high pressure warmth, and the tentacles.

79

Sabre remained drifting all the rest of that day. He may have been remembering kinder seas, and even considering whether to ignore the urge that pulled him northwards, and turn and swim once more towards Scotland; for here he was in a place he did not wish to be, and worse still he was alone.

On the face of the tilting Atlantic there were few eyes to notice the progress of the solitary killer whale with the Gulf Stream at his tail. The call of the northern ocean pulled relentlessly, and after his pause, with the fires once more fresh within him, Sabre pushed himself into the mighty hills of water that were lifted by the cool breeze that blew from the high plateau of Greenland.

To the east of Iceland Sabre met another lonely whale. Like a submarine it appeared on the edge of the killer whale's sonar range. Soft voiced, it was swimming at right angles to Sabre's northerly course. Blowing at the surface, he waited, and watched for the giant crossing his path.

Sabre had never seen a Blue whale before, and he might never meet another. The largest animals that ever lived, not excluding the great reptiles, they once, before the explosive harpoon, roamed the seas of the world in many thousands. Over a hundred feet in length, these stately monarchs of the animal kingdom migrated north and south, east and west, with the krill-rich currents. Then mankind learnt of these most valuable of creatures, and the slide began.

The whale approaching Sabre was an old cow, who had miraculously survived many many years of commercial whaling; but she had lost all her friends and family to the whalers. First the British, before they forsook the profits of whaling, robbed her of her big bull, and then the Russians and the Japanese took her young. She had escaped the flensing decks, but her only companion was loneliness.

Tall waves threw the sun-light dancing down her body. She had long furrows along her belly and throat. She was a graceful, white flecked, blue giant, with a tiny feminine dorsal fin, and huge tail flukes that drove her effortlessly towards her unknown destiny.

Thus Sabre, one of the ocean's war-lords, met one of its few remaining queens. She slid into view, rolling a big eye, until she saw the killer whale. Her song stopped, and she swept out her long elegant flippers, sending her into a slow turn. Her flukes, almost as wide as Sabre's length, wafted powerfully upwards. Sabre felt the eddying blast of water, and watched the organic mountain twist gently away.

Sailors of old, drifting in calm northern waters, heard the song of whales; humpbacks, blues and fins, through the hulls of their ships. In their superstitions they called the singing whales the 'Ghosts of the Deep'. They imagined the sounds were the voices of long dead sailors drowned at sea. Now, many years on, the 'drowned sailors' are growing quiet, perhaps accepting their fate at last. The great baleen whales are becoming scarce, and their voices in the ocean infrequent. It is a tragic irony that they have been called 'Ghosts of the Deep', as their song is banished farther and farther towards the poles by the loud-voiced harpoon. On the blue whale and her kind the sun was setting.

Sabre followed the blue cow for several miles towards the evening sun. After her initial fright she grew more relaxed, and ignored the menacing black and white killer whale following close behind. Her mouth opened, and her chin ballooned, making her look even larger, as she drove herself through rich clouds of plankton. Her mouth closed, and murky water pushed out of her smiling jaws as she swallowed. She resumed her song. Sabre followed, perhaps learning her secrets, or maybe just over-awed by her size.

The sun kissed into a glowing ocean, and both whales became encased in a halo of phosphorescence. Sabre left her then to the peace she deserved, and turned back to his own journey; his quest for the north.

The sounds of waves breaking on the shores of Iceland were left behind. Again the floor began to drop away, and Sabre's sonar returned the buzzing echoes of limitless distance.

There was no longer any night. The sun rose from the sea to its zenith in twelve hours, and then fell back for the next twelve, but never quite reached the horizon and the new dawn. Midnight was like the southern dusk. Sabre was in the ocean of the midnight sun; he had crossed the Arctic circle.

Now there was no Pole star to guide him; instead he followed the feeble warm currents pushing from the south-west, and the fresh taste of cold water seeping down from the ice.

The sea was still full of enemies for the lonely bull. Even his own kind had turned against him. He met them by chance as he cruised around the shallows of Iceland's coast. Small playful cows met him with their exciting songs, and stroked enticingly down his broad flanks. In a surge of joy, and some almost forgotten memory, he danced with them in the waves, chasing them and nipping at their tails. But always the bulls arrived: big amber-eyed males with thunder in their swim. He

82

fought briefly with them all, but the result was always the same: a high-speed retreat, with tail thrusting him away from the laughing voices of the cows, and the bellowing males. The result was always the same because the bulls had everything to fight for, while Sabre merely protected an empty heart.

Beneath the dusky orange midnight sky Sabre met his first icebergs. A lazy summer swell lifted and rumbled against the sun-worn tide-chipped faces of the bergs. The light played amongst the towering pillars, and long flame-edged shadows stretched away from the bronzed giants to the limits of sight.

Dropping away for a thousand feet the bergs floated towards the south. Many years on, beneath the sun of warmer latitudes, the colossal bergs would fade, wilting away into the sea, until they were smooth-faced 'growlers', rolling ten-ton blocks, in the death-throes of solid existence. Now they were drifting islands with sea birds resting and chattering amongst their crannied heights, and cod shoals swimming in the deep blue at a hundred feet. On the water-line seals rested, after many days of travelling against the strong cold waters of the Arctic Ocean.

Two days later, beneath a red-painted sky, Sabre arrived at the fringe of the ice-cap. The pack-ice reached about him. He slid into the blue channels, gazing at the colour-patterned waters, feeling the smooth-faced blocks stroke along his belly, and listening to the silence of the north.

Here, where Forkfin before him had grown huge and hard, Sabre met the sun-drenched polar seascape. Here, where Forkfin had lost everything, Sabre, with nothing to lose and all to gain, entered into the endless sheets of white waste at the roof of the world.

Perhaps the killer whale could remember kinder times in gentler seas. Times with his parents in the food-rich Scottish waters, or times with the Great School, with the calves and old Forkfin: years of learning, and playing and hunting. Or perhaps he could only remember the moments of horror. And maybe all of this was gone, and he saw only the frozen ice-scape, and the fights and Orion's death were merely scars and the kinder times only weak vestiges of warmth in his belly. Whatever he thought, whatever he felt, he pushed into the channels and began his summer amongst the ice.

From the blood-red horizon of the dusk-dawn the sun traversed its tireless path, now touching the clouds in a splayed spectrum, then climbing up higher, its own glare washing away the colours. When it ultimately waned, it deepened the light into great smouldering sky-fires which, during the summer, would never completely be extinguished.

The bergs, towering peaks above the sheet-ice, were ablaze with their own fleeting transience of colour. From the dark purple deep beneath them, to turquoise where the shelves sloped down into the surface, their faces caught the sun's mood: now blushing red with deep dark lines etching the sheer walls, then clear white streaked with rich veins of blue.

To this ever changing multi-hued world Sabre had travelled thousands of miles; searching for something, always calling and waiting, and driving his aching body on as the urge deep inside him grew, and the loneliness became bitter and supplied its own ache.

Now there was this bewildering ice-desert with its bursting colours, and no sign or sound of whatever had pulled him north. So the lonely bull waited and listened for voices drifting on the tide. All summer long he called and searched and hunted and waited, listening for replies, willing himself on under the swelling sun, while the ice-floes shrank, and big cracks opened deeper and deeper towards the Pole.

Sabre was one of countless visitors to the summer pack ice. As the melt ate away the floes the cap shrank, and the seas bloomed with krill and plankton. Even as the sun had crept above spring's horizon, and winter's ghosts were still clinging to the dim-lit crevasses in the white cliffs, the first birds had arrived. Within a month, when great shadows lanced across the orange-tinted plains, and the thaw had begun, huge flocks had flown in from southern tundra regions and the temperate latitudes. When Sabre first stole into the channels the air was already full of the chatter of birds, and their twisting diving flight.

Here and there a polar bear plodded across the floes or fished, quick-pawed, in the gaps between the drifting pack-ice. They travelled, sometimes singly, sometimes in pairs with cubs, far away from the nearest land masses of Greenland and the Arctic islands, drawn by the welling sounds and smells of life in the wastes.

Seals came to breed, collecting on chosen sloping shelves above the gurgling surge of the tide. Plump and shining in the sun, they waited, while the impatient kick of life inside them throbbed in readiness and urgency.

Occasionally alone, though more often in herds of many individuals, walruses hauled out on to the drifting slabs of ice. Beneath their immense weight the ice creaked and groaned, tilting as they jostled one another for the most favoured positions. Old adults surrounded the herds and, seemingly short-sightedly but with constant thoroughness, they scanned the plains and the sea for polar bears and killer whales, their only natural predators. If the smell or sound of a ship came too close the old ones led the herd away across the wastes: battalions of grey-brown mammals forming an undulating acre of tusked fat, striving for the enemy-free hunting grounds of the far north.

Men came; men with clubs, or men in fast ice-breaking ships armed with harpoon cannons. Men from Canada and North America, walking out over the ice, hunting for the harp and fur seals. Men smashing the skulls of the white cubs, and ripping their skins away, leaving the mothers to whimper over the bloody remains left lying there on the ice. Ships came from Russia skirting the edge of the pack ice, seeking the tell-tale plumes of whales spouting amongst the drifts. Then there would be the explosive cough of a gun, loud in the clear Arctic air, and the snaking of rope in the wake of grenade-headed spears; the submarine screams of whales: another lost friend; and another.

A smudge of smoke in the northern sky, blood-stains in the sea and on the white ice: men came to the Arctic to hunt in the richness of the quick cool summer.

Now the northern ocean was full of noise: flashing white bergs, shimmering, splitting and crackling under the sun; avalanches of ice splinters sizzling into the sea; mad ice-echoes, weird sounds rebounding and distorting across the wastes.

When the sun was low, during the quiet hours, the birds rested on their cold nests. There was the chuck, chuck of wavelets lapping against the channel walls, the hissing of ice-laden winds swirling on the planes, the throaty growl of a polar bear roused from slumber by playful cubs, and somewhere near the edge of the sheet-ice a big black Right whale blew, his cavernous voice carried on the breeze far across the frozen desert.

The shadows grew shorter as noon drew near, and the sun whitened in the intense blue sky. Ice rolled and tumbled and crashed into the sea creating shock waves which seared across the planes. Splits formed, veining the Polar cap with blue, shattering mountains of ice in their path. Million ton blocks dropped and slid into the ocean. Spouts of water lifted hundreds of feet, hung there, churning and raging, and then fell tumbling and boiling upon the new bergs.

The birds dipped or dived into the waves, or screeched and proclaimed their territory with twisting acrobatics, and spread-winged abuse.

The seals slept through it all, until the scar-necked males barked their orders, or hunger drove the colonies into the gloom beneath the ice to hunt out the fish.

Sabre the hunter stole beneath the white ceiling. He weaved his way between long spears and pinnacles of ice, dropping deep into the sea. He hid in submarine caves, and listened to the pulse of the Arctic. The living sounds; the heavy walk of a polar bear close by, a walrus feeding on the sea floor, churning up the silt with his tusks, the plop, plop, plop of a flock of birds diving for krill, a cod shoal swishing beneath him, the seals playing in the surf; these sounds held his quick brain. He focussed, he echo-located, he calculated. Then he moved towards his target. Death sweeping on thrusting flukes from the deep, the ping of his sonar, a blast of water, a flash of white or a dark smudge just before the end; thus he hunted and killed and grew in the summer drifts.

Sabre was now twenty-six feet long. His flippers were huge and round: his dorsal almost six feet tall, and his flukes wide and curved. He bore scars; some long and thin from rock and ice, some grey and twisting from battles with squid and conger and bull killer whales. He was extremely powerful. Fish, bird and mammal, all became his victims: the sweeping arcing dorsal, the slam of his tail, or just the finality of his jaws: whichever way, the end was the same: few escaped.

Hidden by the ice until the last furious moments Sabre gave his prey little chance. He could herd the seals against the sheer walls of icebergs, or trap them in chosen channels: arenas too wide for quick-flippered retreat. Whichever way the seals turned the tall fin rose, water cascading from its trailing edge. They saw a dark swirl, perhaps the cold sparkle in his eyes, or the pink of his gaping mouth: and no more.

In the diffuse light of evening, the killer whale found shelves washed by the gentle swell. He pushed himself up on to these ice-beaches so that almost a third of his body was above the water. He rested there and slept, and waited for the Arctic's heartbeat to grow in intensity with the rising sun.

His skin crinkled and greyed when exposed to the air and the sun, but the ice-laden spray cooled him, and the waves bathed him, surging and caressing.

In the morning he would be woken by a bird pecking nonchalantly at his tough hide, a seal barking from away across the ice-fields, the bursting thudding and crashing of the wastes, or just the intense ache of loneliness within him, and the desire, the urge, to swim with his own kind.

He pushed himself off his shelf, blowing loudly in the sudden flood of cold and tickle of bubbles. Diving, he passed beneath the ice and stared up at his ceiling. Some-times silver and white where it was thinnest, sometimes blue and dense, or fissured and cracked, descending im-mense into the dullness far below. Sabre searched beneath the thin ice. A smudge of colour above him, a deepening of shade, gave away the position of some luckless creature resting under the glare of the morning sun. The killer whale rose, crashing through the ice, kicking, cartwheeling and falling, headfirst, towards his shocked prey.

The brief summer drew on: the summer of the easy hunt; the summer of ever intensifying loneliness. Sabre worked his way towards the east, across the endless day at the roof of the northern hemisphere; killing or maim-ing all in his path, leaping and snapping at fleet-winged terns and skuas, launching himself high above the sur-face. And all the time there was the cold around him, and the frozen bitter ache within; torturing, driving him to kill; forcing him to head-crash into the unfeeling walls of ice. He called; pleading, painful long notes; but they bounced back at him, echoing mockingly from every direction: and it was a cold sound, frozen like the Arctic wastes. So he stopped calling and merely listened.

His great heart lurched whenever he heard the voices of whales drifting across the ice-desert. But he heard no killer whales. The whispering voices of the beluga whales tormented him, for he understood little of their language. Once he swam with these white whales for their company. He frightened them at first, appearing, ghostly, from the gloom. They bolted and merged into the ice, shielding their grey calves from him. But then they sensed no menace from the huge killer whale. They swam towards him, forming a white halo around him.

He stayed with them many hours, bathed in their peace. They curled over the surface together, and gave him, for those few hours, a sad comfort. Then he grew hungry and left them, diving deep for the cod shoals. When he returned to the light, they were gone with their songs and their calves and their warmth.

The appalling risks had to end. The deep, deep dives into the abyss, the blind swimming in submarine caves, dodging, by use of sonar, jagged swords of ice, the back-wrenching battering into sheet-ice too thick to break, and travelling too far into the north as autumn fell, while the channels froze in his wake.

Great flocks of birds took to the air and beat urgently southwards. The sun now sank beneath the horizon for longer and longer each day, until there were a few hours of genuine darkness in each twenty-four, and dusk became divided from the dawn. Whining snow-laden blizzards tore across the plains, and the ice-cap began to fall into a frozen twilight. Quietly, under angry skies, the polar bears plodded back towards land, and the seals took their pups south. The bursting richness of summer faded with the sun. The ocean humped, and the drift-ice heaved and throbbed: winter clawed its way into the Arctic.

The killer whale ignored the signs. He heaved himself out on to the sloping ledges, and listened to the wind moaning in the heights of towering bergs. Another risk; a moment closer to disaster. Sabre lay there in the half light, minutes from catastrophe.

Spraylash

THE LEDGE TREMBLED. Sabre awoke instantly, but the quivering soon died away and the killer whale drifted once again into sleep. Twice more the beach beneath him shook, waking him each time. The ledge tilted a little, leaving him beached higher, but again he fell asleep unaware or uncaring of the danger: the unforgivable insult to the high Arctic.

Above him stretched a great overhanging cliff of blue ice. Throughout the summer the cliff's supports had dripped away under the constant warmth of the sun. A crack, fierce and harsh in its closeness, shook Sabre awake. In reflex he kicked and twisted on to his side. It was enough to save him from being crushed beneath the full mass of the ice-fall, but no more. It caught him hard in the flank, smashing his ribs, and blasting the light from his eyes.

It seemed as though he swam in a cloud for hours. He heard Forkfin's voice far away, and then the pain broke through his dream, and he saw the ice; sharp ice falling upon him; blue ice reaching out of the deep towards him; mountains of ice toppling around him ... then the cloud fell across his eyes, and he dreamt of Orion falling on his last journey into the darkness, and he was with him, watching his father's red belly all the way down into the abyss. And his mother far above them, singing for them both, pleading; calling them back to the surface. Then he was on his own on the sea floor, and giant squid were enveloping him with their tentacles, and gouging at his flank with their horny beaks. Pain pierced the nightmare and again he saw the ice.

When the ice-fall had caught Sabre it had not thrown him into the water, but had pushed him higher on to the shelf. This saved his life, for had he dropped into the sea he would have drowned. He lay on his side, while a trickle of blood ran from an angry wound near his blow hole. His whole body trembled, and in his tortured unconsciousness he cried out and shook. Each time he woke he moaned weakly, calling for help, but only the ice heard his plea.

For the first time in his life the cold pierced into his heart. He wanted to drop back into the ocean. He moved, and the pain in his chest stabbed him into another unconscious hallucination.

Now he was in the sea of the Hebrides, and a warm current pushed into his face. The white sand was sun-dappled beneath him, and big red clouds of plankton hung and wafted in the water winds. Kelp stroked down his belly, and a beautiful blue whale sang to him, and wrapped her huge soft flippers about him. She bucked her great floppy body, and carried him towards the southern warmth.

He lay there for a long time, his skin greying in the cold air, and the blood trickling down his flank on to the ice. His breathing was shallow and hoarse; his chest quivered; the ice began to take him.

A tightness in his chest brought him back to reality, and the desperate futility of his position. He just wanted to fall into the comforting sea, and swim far away from the north, and find some killer whales to hunt and play with; to share their song, to feel their pulsing life.

He rolled on to his belly and the shock of agony almost killed him. His next spout was tainted with red. The cold pulled him back into its deceitful sleep. The sun shone above him, and kept him, barely, alive. The ice beneath him sapped at his warmth, and his strength ebbed into the soulless Arctic wastes. He lay in a pool of frozen blood, and horrors gripped his mind. Birds pecked eagerly at his wound. He moaned and fell a little deeper into the numbing trance of the cold.

Hanging on the edge of oblivion Sabre fought for his life. Talons of pain clawed him in and out of consciousness, while the ice pulled at him, tempting him with its frozen peace.

The ice shelf tipped slightly and the killer whale slid into the water. He rolled, belly up, and began to sink. Down, down, away from light, away from life, into the warm blanketing darkness. Like Orion ... pink belly upwards.

Something made Sabre kick his tail, weakly, and his flippers stroked him upright. The nausea or the pain, the burning in his wound, the heaviness in his chest, or a sudden terrifying memory of squid down there in the ocean, kept him conscious, as he reached his head into the air, and gasped and gulped in the coolness. The last feeble threads of life strained.

He called, weak sobbing noises, and listened to the mocking ice-echoes. He sank below the sheet ice and screamed. The urgent plea reached far out across the Arctic ocean, and many ears heard it. A Greenland Right whale heard it, and could recognise only the horror it bore. Seals heard it and fled, for they recognised the language of killer whales. A walrus heard the scream, and quickly climbed out of the sea, using his tusks to haul himself high on to the ice, for he too hated and feared that voice ... But no killer whales heard his distress.

Slowly, very slowly Sabre beat his great flukes, and nudged himself towards the wall of a leaning blue berg. He bit into a jut of ice and held on to stop himself sinking. His energy was almost spent, cold beckoned with gentle sleep. He screamed and bellowed, and thought of Scottish seas, and screamed again. A convulsion tore open his wound, and he bled into the merciless sea. A wave washed across his back, sending water gurgling into his vent-hole. He coughed, and the white pain scorched in his chest, and again he screamed.

And then he had no more strength to scream, so he sobbed for help, and began to lose his fight. The threads started to break. The white-hot agony was numbing. Frozen death closed its grip, but still he breathed, and with each expulsion of air he cried out into the ice.

Many miles to the south, prowling the edge of the pack-ice, was a pack of eleven killer whales. They had been there for over a week, swimming slowly west, ambushing the animals escaping from the autumn cold on the cap. At night they swam a mile away from the drifts to the safety of deep clear water. Dawn and the plop and splash of life drew them back. Now it was noon, and they crept amongst the floating islands: hunting.

The pack's leader was a small young bull. He had replaced the old master, who had been dead for half a year. The young male had little discipline over the others, and they mistrusted his careless weak-voiced command. They were all cows, and only two of them swam with calves.

One cow, just twenty feet long, with proud broad white markings, hung far to the rear of the pod. She listened to their hunting calls as the bull led them into the drift ice, and she played in the short waves of the autumn sea, ignoring the pod. Her name was Spraylash. She was uncomfortable here in the Arctic ocean, and she longed to be in her home waters: deep, calm Scandinavian fjords, and the broad expanse of ocean between Norway's glaciated coast and the Faroe Isles.

The young cow felt the tremor of a shoal of fish move beneath her. She dived with a long elegant roll and cut into them. It was then that she heard the scream.

Instantly she stopped, while the fish flashed silver, like sparks, about her. They fled and she was left in the calm, listening to the voices of the polar cap.

Another scream, Sabre's last, weak, but steeped with pain, trembled in her sensitive ears, and her huge heart lurched. She recognised the voice of a bull killer whale in desperate need of help; a bull who was dying somewhere out there in the white maze. She screamed back at him, telling him she was coming, if he could just hold on until she found him. Then she rose to the surface and drew in deep breaths, preparing herself for the ordeal. She dived again and thrust her great body beneath the ice, calling as she built up speed.

The leader heard her go and he called for her to return, but she ignored him. Twice more he called, and then he forgot about her. Neither he nor any member of his pod ever saw Spraylash again.

She galloped beneath the drifts in the direction of those two weak screams. She cried out, again and again, willing the dying whale to answer her, to tell her where he

was. There was no reply, so she raced on; calling, pleading, crying. She was forced to rise for air, and she crashed
through the thin ice and gasped quick deep breaths,
numbing her aching chest. She launched herself forward,
diving under the hanging walls of ice, and then back up
to the light to breathe, and to listen for the bull's voice.

Sabre could not hear her, he could no longer even hear
the waves washing over his back. The nausea had gone;
the pain had gone: his mind had sunk into numbness.
Hope drifted away, and left behind the certainty of endless sleep. Soft memories helped him into the coma ... He
was in Scottish seas again, and he could taste the tang of
heather in the breeze, and feel the force of the rip tides in
his face ... Something, not hope, not fear, nor whisper
through the sea; but something made him bite harder
into his purchase on the ice. His body hung limply,
uselessly, beneath him, but still his blow-hole was in the
air, and still he sobbed.

Spraylash sped deeper into the high Arctic. She called
all the way; she strove and thrust her great flukes,
crashing through the ice, and blowing hot spouts on to
the faces of the bergs. She heard no sound from the bull,
so she thrust herself on, screaming for him to answer her:
surging beneath the white ceiling.

The ice broke. Sabre took as deep a breath as he could
manage and fell away from the surface, tail first into the
gloom. A trail of silver bubbles streamed from his blow-
hole. They carried his last call; deep, lost, without hope.
The bubbles burst at the surface and there was no more
sound.

She heard him, and again her great heart quickened.
She turned towards him and kicked, and thrust beneath
the bergs, the clear Arctic ocean churning in her slip-

stream. Down, down into the sea, down towards the call. She turned, echo-located, and heard something huge above her. She rose.

There in the greyness she found him. Great sleeping whale falling into the sea: beautiful, tall finned, black and white bull, dropping towards her. She swept beneath him and pushed into his belly, and felt his bulk weighing down on her back: unmoving, unconscious whale, magnificent heavy bull. With an effort she lifted him to the surface.

They remained there together a long while, a small pocket of clinging life amongst the bergs. Sabre drew shallow breaths, and Spraylash held him above the waves. She spoke to him, soft voiced, telling him that she was there, that he was safe; but he did not hear her, and his eyes remained dull and cold. But something must have pierced the coma, for the next day he whimpered very quietly, just once, lifted a huge flipper and rested it across her back.

The cold left his heart and sleep replaced the unconscious haze, but cruel nightmares still shook his body, making him cry out, as the agony in his chest returned with the fading numbness. After several days, resting in the same place, the first glimmer of sense returned, and his eyes rolled, blurred and tired. His gaze took in the surrounding ice and the grey sky, and the bubbles swirling in the blueness. Then Spraylash swam out from beneath him, and he saw her wide soft back, and as she blew in front of him, he could see her white-dashed body, round and strong, feminine and ripe. She turned and faced him. She nudged carefully into his chin with her long smiling mouth, and he saw the sparkling glow in her eyes. Then she moved back beneath him, and he felt himself lifted above the sea. He breathed, deeply, the cold left him, and he wrapped his flippers around her warm back.

He slept, and no more fierce dreams came to torment him. Whenever he was awoken by the pain in his side he heard Spraylash's calm song coaxing him back to peaceful slumber.

The wastes froze about them. Thin ice formed over the channels in the diffuse pale blue of evening. The freeze inched southwards, leaving the whales back on the white plains, a tiny oasis in the high Arctic. Spraylash heard and felt the encroaching winter, and watched violet streaks etch across the fading sky. She knew that they must leave that frozen place, and she thought once more of her Norwegian coast beneath its autumn glow. Somehow she had to escape with her bull, before they were trapped for ever in that forgotten corner of the northern hemisphere. She called to Sabre, and nudged him forward. He understood and trusted her, so he followed, sweeping his flukes, while a mist of pain clouded his eyes. But their retreat was frozen over, and he was too weak to force himself through the ice. Spraylash broke through it, every yard of the way, blasting a path for her bull. He stopped frequently, resting his chin upon her softness, while he gathered enough strength for the next painful sweep of his tail. She held him, she head-slammed a passage for them both, or leapt and crashed down on to thick ice. She called and pulled at him, as the ice grew thicker and cut into her belly, sapping her great strength. And all the while Sabre trusted her, unable to help, and watched her beautiful body working for them both.

They came upon a long ridge of ice, an unbreakable slab, reaching far down into the sea. They had to pass beneath it. Spraylash pulled at Sabre and he followed her, falling in her slipstream. The colossal pressure beat down on his chest, and the old agony seared through his body. He cried out until he felt her beneath him, pushing him on under the massive plateau of dark ice. He tried; he beat his flukes all the way to the end of the ridge, but then he lost consciousness. Spraylash hauled him to the surface, sometimes pushing from beneath, sometimes grasping for a hold with her flippers across his enormous back, and then bucking her aching body, lifting them both towards the light.

There followed another long struggle across the seemingly endless sheet as she crashed her way through. She tried too hard for too long, hurting herself, exhausting her starving body: but she got them out of the ice.

They felt the ocean's lift, and heard the drift-ice fall away to their rear. Spraylash pushed her head above the water and stared back at the cap, just once. In front of them lay a few big ice-bergs, and then no more: empty blue ocean all the way to Norway.

She was hungry, and the cold was starting to eat into her. After a summer's feeding in the Arctic both she and Sabre had built up large deposits of blubber to insulate them from the cold, and to act as food when the hunt became less successful. Now she had been nearly a fortnight without any food, and Sabre much longer. The cold had worked away at their fat, and they were both exhausted. She knew she had to find prey in this suddenly quiet, lifeless ocean.

On that first day out of the ice-fields she caught a seal, deep in the sea. She brought the carcass to Sabre and pushed it into his mouth. He turned it over a few times and then gulped it down whole. The next day she caught three guillemots, and took them all to the bull sleeping at the surface. The birds had been diving and chasing after cod nearly two hundred feet down. She heard their plunge into the waves, and their winged descent towards the shoal. Sabre wolfed down the hot flesh, and Spraylash left him there and dived to find the cod.

Slowly Sabre repaired; his ribs set crudely but strong, and the internal damage, the bleeding and bruising, righted itself. The wound on his flank healed over until it was just another scar. His mind took much longer to recover. For a month after leaving the ice he slept or swam, weakly, in the direction Spraylash showed him. In a daze he accepted the food that his huntress brought.

The ice had nearly killed Sabre, and pulled him down towards its fatal slumber. His blubber and enormous strength, together with an urge deep in his guts, had given him time. Though the time would have been cruel and useless had it not been for the she-whale. Spraylash was never to forget the day she heard a scream from the edge of the ice.

Sense returned slowly to the killer whale's brain. At first he felt only tremendous relief that there was now only infrequent nausea, or pain, or nightmare. There was no longer helplessness or despair. He had given up hope; come a heart-beat away from giving up life; and now he was swimming free. No more bergs, no ice, or thousands of lonely feet of Arctic ocean. Beneath him now, nursing him or hunting for him, singing and calling to him, nudging him with her softness and showing him what he must do, was the beautiful cow whale. With

100

her constant attention, with her gifts of food, with the hope and care in her voice and the warmth she gave him, sense and purpose returned to Sabre.

Norway

SPITSBERGEN, BEAR ISLAND and the Arctic wastes lay far behind them, like the dreadful memory. The Shelf was beneath them now, and sounds from Norway's coast rumbled through the sea.

Sabre was fully repaired, but tired after the long haul from the north. He welcomed the shallow-water rollers, and the abundant coast-bound fish shoals. He started to hunt again, diving down with Spraylash, all the way to the floor, calling to her and linking up with her sonar: hunting through the deep.

Cumulous clouds billowed above them. The whales lifted their heads above the swells to watch their passing. On the southern horizon they saw land. North Cape, and behind that, fading into the tired glow of evening, the mountains of Norway. Spraylash was home. After long journeys through adolescence and many lost friends, she was in waters she knew so well. And she had brought with her, to this sea of her calf-hood, the big bull, Sabre.

Closer to the coast they heard the waves clawing and crashing against the Cape's rocks. The snow-peaked, glacier-carved mountains loomed up high in the sky, red and brooding in the early winter sun.

Two weeks later they crossed the Arctic Circle and were in the waters of southern Norway. Here amongst the fjords, they stayed all winter: two killer whales, together on a lonely coast. Beautiful lonely coast: beautiful lonely times: together.

By day they hunted: perfect, lethal hunters. Sabre showed Spraylash how to stalk their prey by hiding in a wave: swimming along the roller, closing the gap until the moment came for them to turn and fall down the cascades, right on top of their unsuspecting victims. They fell together into the troughs, kicking up the spray.

Spraylash took Sabre into the fjords, and showed him the calm clear waters. He listened to her sonar sweep down and far away, and the echoes return crisp and clear, undistorted by tide races and the disturbance of the wave-smashed coast.

Here, in the long night, they came together. The setting sun would find them playing, briskly, at the surface, throwing red bow-waves out across the fjord. They nipped at each other, touching, splashing, leaping and happy. An osprey, on silent wings, watched their frolic, and in the woods at the fjord's edge a red squirrel heard the splashing, and curled himself tighter in his pine nest.

Sabre lunged himself at her whiteness, but she tore away; coyly: again and again. He chased after her, swept beneath her, and tried to grasp her with his great flippers and pull her down into the sea. And then it was right, and they curved away into the darkness; fins clasped; together: a thousand feet down into the ocean: hovering in the mid-deeps, in the silence, in the night. Perfect, happy whales.

In the turquoise waters etching towards the glaciers the killer whales spent the short winter. The fjord shores, crowded with dense forests of pine, lay beneath a soft blanket of snow. Except for a few pockets of life ruffling the white forest face the land slept. A hawk, sharp-eyed, dropped on closed wings towards a smudge of movement in the snow: a kick, a spurt of white, a muffled noise reaching through the forest, and a tiny mammal lay clasped in its talons. A triumphant screech soared above the trees.

High up in the mountains the mantle of ice grew thicker, and the glaciers creaked under the tremendous weight. The noise of storms at sea penetrated the silence of the fjords: malignant fury out there on the ocean, but here, beneath the forests and the tall mountains, the barely moving tide bathed the killer whales in peace.

Spring shook the land and the sea. The glaciers cracked and groaned, and avalanches of rock and ice rumbled through the mountains. The rivers were white with melt water. They churned and foamed far out into the fjords. The evergreens shrugged off their coats of snow, and slowly put on their delicate light green trimmings. Salmon flooded in from the sea, chased by seals. The killer whales found them both. Spraylash fed ravenously on spring's flood of protein, quenching a fierce hunger welling within her.

With the coming of longer days the fjords grew busy. Man floated out over the deep waters. The high-pitched whine of propellers sang through the waves, nets crashed, big diesel motors throbbed: man fished and hunted, and crowded upon the sea.

Sabre and Spraylash heard the increasing bustle, and left the fjords to those other hunters of the surface.

Amongst the islands of southern Norway they spent the early summer: a rich Scandinavian summer, with an intense blue sky, and white cumulus clouds billowing, anvil and galleon shaped, on the horizon. The sea was full of Cetacean noises; the screeching of porpoise schools and huge pods of pilot whales, jet black and slow, drifting close to the shore. A few big baleen whales passed by a long way to seaward, and once they heard a pack of killer whales to the north. They listened to the calls they understood so well, and then forgot them, as they disappeared in the remote hills of water to the north-west.

Under blazing summer skies Sabre and Spraylash swam farther and farther out to sea, until the sounds of the coast were mere murmurs in the night. The abundant Norwegian sea fed them, they had each other's company, and it seemed there could be little more to desire. And yet the ice and Norway had given them more than each other, and now that extra being was making its kicking presence felt deep inside Spraylash.

Possibly the she-whale understood what was happening, and the movements in her belly caused her no alarm, and she just cried out in reflex, causing Sabre to charge up to her side and call to her soothingly, protectively. It was also possible that Spraylash understood little, and Sabre less, about the new life growing within her, the new life that would link them together even more intensely than now. Whether they understood or not, Spraylash was a little frightened as they moved westwards into the North Sea, and Sabre tasted, for the first time in almost two years, a distant hint of the British Isles. Something instinctive was making him lead Spraylash to the seas of his calf-hood. It was not the call of his kind for there were no other killer whales here. It was probably the comfortable feel of the waters he knew, and perhaps above all it was the call of his memory.

Glowchin

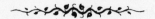

THE LAST TWO HUNDRED miles were slow. Travelling no more than five miles a day, the two whales dawdled across the sea. Repeatedly, sometimes for long periods, Spraylash called out and stopped, resting her heavy body in the oily swell. While Sabre nudged her gently, her big round belly rippled, and she spouted continuously and strained. The spasm passed, it always passed, and they moved off again: two shadows, side by side …

The island sprawl of Orkney loomed out of the sea, at first like a smudge of smoke on the horizon, then round, low-lying mounds showed above the waves, heather-clad and purple, beneath a September sky. The taste of peat in the bays welcomed them, and the boom and crash of the foaming Scottish seas reminded Sabre, fleetingly, of those other days, before the Great School, before the ice, and before Spraylash.

The she-whale heaved herself around the islands with a degree of lost grace which betrayed her effort. She no longer hunted, and Sabre killed for them both, as once she had done in the high north.

It happened in the night, a cloudless, mistless night, with a full moon directly overhead. Spraylash arched her body once, twice, three times … The tail appeared, glinting in the moonlight; the cow rolled on to her side, and in one deliberate movement she formed a great arched bow

106

and straightened ... The calf was born, a cow calf, with large white markings like her mother, which out-shone the wave crests. Her name was Glowchin.

The little whale gasped in the cool Atlantic air, while Spraylash nudged her along the surface. Sabre encircled them both, calling to them; soothing, reassuring noises in the darkness.

The same thing that had baffled Sabre on the day of his birth now confused his calf: the scents on the breeze of bitter-sweet heather, the staleness of bird-colonies and weed thrown up on the shore: the endless chuck and swish of the waves, the gurgling bubbling crests; her mother's gentle song, and the pulsing protective swim of the big bull.

Instinctively mother and father knew what to do. They moved across the night sea slowly, almost drifting where the tide would take them. Spraylash rolled, so that her broad white belly was above the waves. Glowchin had not yet learnt to suckle from her mother while they were submerged, without swallowing sea-water, but on the surface a gallon of rich milk flushed rapidly into the calf's eager mouth.

Sabre swam beneath them, emitting brief bursts of sound, and listening for anything that might mean danger. There was nothing to cause him concern, so he dived down into the sea to hunt. He caught a skate on the rocky floor, and brought the great winged fish to his mate at the surface. She gulped it down ravenously while he looked, bewildered, at the tiny shape hiding beneath her fore-flipper. Spraylash moved quietly, exposing, for a proud moment, the cow calf for Sabre's gaze. The bull's stare took in her tiny whale shape, her six feet of freshness. She had as much white as black on her body, and a broad grey 'saddle' behind her hooked dorsal. The calf lifted her head into the air and spouted, while Sabre moved effortlessly beneath her. He saw her tail splash clumsily in the swell, and her quizzical eyes sparkle in the moonlight. Then she bolted after Spraylash and swam at her side, mimicking her mother's every move.

Long after the dawn, with the sun behind them, Sabre swam in the slipstream of his family, watching their slow progress and listening to their quiet voices. Something stirred deep within him, and all through the autumn day he watched them, and called to them, and with his voice he led them through the same seas where Orion had led him and his mother.

The weather remained idyllic for the rest of the month; a Scottish Indian summer, as rare as it was perfect. The soft breeze from the west remained and kept the frost out of the air at night. The sea rolled peacefully about the islands, so that Glowchin had a gentle world in which to build up strength before the turbulence of winter. Even Cape Wrath slept, as Sabre led them into the North Minch, reassuringly calm beneath an autumn sky.

When at last winter broke, the killer whales had drifted far to the south. On their port flank lay Ireland's green hills. To their starboard was that infinity of emptiness which is an ocean sky. The surface was lit by a harsh winter glare, the sun travelling low in the sky through the shortening days. There was no food on the surface, and Sabre was forced to dive to the floor. There he found skate and conger, or a shoal of cod floating across the twilit regions of the sea.

A wildness began to build along this Atlantic coast, so Sabre led Spraylash and her calf further into the south.

They spent December off North Cornwall, with the sound of long ocean rollers breaking upon the wide beaches. Here Sabre found a seal colony at the end of the breeding season. In a single day he killed three; two cows and a big beach-master, snatched from the deep water, beneath a reef stretching away from the colony beach. They did not stay long in the area. Perhaps the seals became wiser, for Sabre found the hunting increasingly difficult. Or he might have remembered another day, long ago, when Orion had stayed too long with a Scottish seal colony.

They moved off down the coast. On calm days Glow-chin chased flatfish across the sandy shallows. She caught very few, and those she did snap into her jaws she dropped. She was still totally dependent on her mother's milk, and the hunting was just a game. Sabre and Spraylash hunted amongst the wrecks and submarine reefs and ate all the flesh they could catch. To them hunting was a vital necessity, and that, together with keeping Glowchin fed and safe, was all there could be in these wintry seas. That, and brief moments alone together, deep in the sea, while Glowchin slept in the peaceful swell.

Red-Eye

B Y MID-WINTER the killer whales were in the central
reaches of the Bay of Biscay, with six thousand
feet of water beneath them and stormy leaden
skies above. Strong gusting westerlies pushed the waters
of the Bay against the land mass of southern Europe,
resulting in a violently arching sea. It was an endless
battle, swimming into green walls of water, with the
shock of thousands of tons of ocean passing over their
backs. Glowchin grew strong, suckling whenever she
could from Spraylash, who rarely denied the calf her
milk. The adult whales had thick layers of blubber to
insulate them from the cold, and now in these times of
rough seas and poor hunting, they drew on their deposits
of fat without undue harm. Spraylash grew a little lean,
having to supply her calf with nourishment as well as
herself. But spring and a plethora of food was not far
away. In the meantime Sabre brought her squid from the
sea floor, and any fish he could find. Presently they came
to the shallows of the Spanish coast. The sea was warmer
here, though puckered by rains, but it was calmer, and
they rested after the strenuous crossing of the Bay.

He came, ferocious, out of the rocky seas. Red-Eye,
Sabre's old enemy in the Great School, swept towards
the astonished bull, with rage in his swim and death on
his mind. Ever since the day of his exile by Forkfin,

110

Red-Eye had roamed the North Atlantic; a rogue, a psychopath amongst his kind, killing and maiming all in his path, driving himself further and further beyond the edge of sanity with each new cruel day. Other killer whales shunned him, for he was a crazed adult bull who had nothing to offer save catastrophe.

By chance Red-Eye had found his old opponent. He had been far down the coast when noises of Sabre and Glowchin at play in the surf had caught his attention. Instantly he accelerated towards them, analysing their voices while the dim fire of recognition gnawed at his mind.

One burst of sonar was enough for Red-Eye to locate with certainty the position of the whales playing by the shore. That echo-locating sound was also enough to alert Sabre, so that he could place himself between Glowchin and the hurtling onslaught. Enormous, the rogue bull charged, tail churning the water into a welter of foam.

The two bulls met, rolling and thrashing in the waves. In that initial attack Sabre came off the worst. It had been so sudden, and Red-Eye had been moving so fast. Badly winded, and with an intense pain in his side, Sabre rolled away down a wave, gasping for air. He had barely enough time to call out a warning to Spraylash, before Red-Eye leapt above him and crashed down, jaws snarling and ripping into his flesh.

The rogue held the initiative in the early stages of the battle, but soon the shock Sabre had felt began to wear off, and was replaced by his own calculating ferocity. He swam away from Spraylash and Glowchin while Red-Eye snapped at his tail. They sped off into the ocean, until Sabre cartwheeled and turned upwards, driving his head hard into Red-Eye's belly.

111

Glowchin hid beneath her mother's flipper, terrified by the noises of violence. Spraylash could only imagine what would ensue if Sabre lost the encounter, and Glowchin simply did not understand. Spraylash did not believe that Sabre could possibly lose, but even so she was tense, and with each fierce noise reaching her ears her heart beat faster, and something tightened deep in her belly.

Night fell, unnoticed, and still the battle raged. Red-Eye fought on because of his madness: Sabre fought on because he now had everything to lose. If he had been alone it might have been different; he might somehow have escaped the rogue, and forgotten the incident. But Spraylash and Glowchin, and all that had happened since the day of the ice-fall, eliminated any possibility of retreat. The two bulls leapt upon each other, and tried to gouge into each other's flesh. They locked jaws and pushed, snarling and gnashing. Each smashed his flukes into the other's face, and they pulled each other down into the sea. The fights from those days in the Great School helped Sabre. Though none had been anything like this, he had learnt Red-Eye's ways in battle. Slowly, painfully, Sabre took the initiative.

Spraylash and her calf smelt blood in the water, and heard the thrashing in the waves, or a dull submarine thud as the two great beasts met. Spraylash felt each shock-wave as though it were a blow to her own body. It did not occur to her that she had once fought like this herself, for Sabre, against an enemy even more unfeeling and vicious than the rogue bull: the ice.

As dawn broke Sabre saw his opponent clearly. Blood gushed from many wounds all over Red-Eye's body. One of the evil eyes was swollen and bleeding, and a big

112

chunk of flesh hung from his chin. In that moment, Sabre realised that he had won, and after one last muscle-tearing attack, he turned, and left the rogue in a red cloud at the surface of the sea.

Spraylash stared, shocked, at the battered whale swimming towards her. Angry wounds ran down his back and flanks, and one of his fore-flippers was torn. He swam on towards her, not even noticing Glowchin hiding beneath her. They bumped together, and she saw the pain in his eyes: swollen, half-seeing eyes. She pushed his head above the waves, and he fell almost immediately into a deep sleep.

Upon the pitching waters of the Bay the three killer whales rode up the west coast of France. Their progress was slow, for often the two females were forced to stop while they lifted the bull's back above the waves, though he needed them less each day. Winter was leaving the northern ocean, and already the shallows held warmth. With the smell of life washing out over the sea, full of promise, the fight with Red-Eye soon faded into scars and memory.

Minch

A<small>T PEACE</small>, Sabre, Spraylash and their calf floated close to the lower Outer Hebrides. The month was May, and the wanderers had returned again to their familiar Scottish waters. The birds had been there for over a month. Long skeins arrived from the south, chattering across the sky, and filling the air-ways with their songs. Now they nested on the sprawl of Atlantic islands, the white-streaked cliffs bearing as much witness to their arrival as the wing-filled air, and their persistent calls drifting far out over the bays.

On land the heather pushed out straggly fresh shoots to feed the sheep and deer and the moor grouse. Rabbits scuttered across the fields, and in the silliness of early summer, fell easy victims to the eagles' talons. Falcons stooped, from high in the sky, to take journey-weary migrants that had come this far; but even as their tired wings carried them over the cliffs of home, the prey-birds' shadows closed with them.

In the ocean, particularly along the shore, the same saga of new life and sudden death was taking place. Seals, with their pups of last autumn, fed on the glut of fish. Porpoises and dolphins curled their quick passage across the green waters of the bays. Basking sharks surfaced like submarines, in the deep water of the sounds, ploughing through the plankton-rich acres. Smaller sharks, blues and tope, sped, hungry-eyed, beneath the waves, their dorsals slicing, like knives, into the air. Salmon and sea-trout flooded into the estuaries, driven, by some mysterious urge, from their feeding arenas in the ocean to the rivers of their birth. The predators capitalised on the seemingly suicidal shoals every inch of the way. There were men with nets: on the high seas, big multi-acre nets, guided by sonar; drift nets in coastal waters; bay and estuary nets on the collecting grounds. Even in the rivers men caught them. Fishermen with fly and lure, questing the exciting lunging leaping power of a fresh run salmon. Poachers with poison, spear and dynamite, desiring only the fat financial rewards for the renowned flesh. Then they had their natural enemies: killer whales, dolphins and porpoises; sharks and seals, and all the sharp-toothed hunters of the sea. The few survivors reaching the flooding rivers and lochs met new enemies: a thick-tailed otter, or an osprey stooping, with incredible accuracy, from the skies. Worst of all there could be drought or disease, and then the whole tortuous journey would have been useless. A few, a precious few, reached the reds, the breeding shallows, by late autumn and laid the foundations for the next cycle, perhaps more successful, usually less so, than the last.

Here, along the crowded coast, Glowchin learnt to hunt properly, finding that it was more than a game, that the taste of flesh was exciting in itself. Though she still relied on her mother's milk, she supplemented her diet with small fish, or scraps of warm seal flesh brought to her by her father. These were happy times for the small family, amongst the tide-races and the sea lochs. But it was the transient touch of happiness; a gift from Nature, beneath the sun. Such days could not last for ever; such happiness can only be fleeting, can only exist until some cruel moment when the world changes, never to be the same again.

Far to the north-west, on the southern coast of Iceland, the bubble of happiness was bursting for a small pod of killer whales, similar in many ways to Sabre and his family. There were five; a bull, two cows and two calves. The bull was a good leader, strong and powerful, though a little young. The two cows trusted and followed him, as they hunted for pilot and small baleen whales in the krill-rich seas. One of the calves was a bull, a year and a half old; the other a cow, who had just come through her first winter.

At first all members of the pod ignored the distant whine of propellers. The screw noises were common enough in these heavily fished seas, and usually they did not come too close. The pod swam on through the waves while the whining grew stronger.

The vessel was not a fisherman, but a whaler: a sleek fast ship equipped with sonar, and an extended harpoon gun platform above the bows. A single high-revolution screw lunged her forwards on her mission. The whaler was based in Iceland, and her main targets were Fin-backs, Sei and other Rorquals; but when these were absent, a few fat bottle-nosed whales or killers could more than pay for the journey. The Icelander flaunted a thin trail of diesel smoke, and cut a sizzling wake as a sighter spotted the blows of the killer whale pod.

They could hear the throbbing of the engine now: a constant thud thud, as the whaler closed on them. The bull rolled down beneath the waves and listened, puzzled, but not unduly concerned. He heard the repeating ping of the whaler's sonar. He emitted a quick chirp of sound, and the echoes told him that the vessel was

116

now very close. Now the leader was alert, though he could not imagine the horrors this vessel bore. He called to his pod, and they swam after him on a course at right angles to the whaler's path.

There was a rush of activity on the Icelander's decks. Two men loaded and primed the gun, while another stood behind them, watching the whales. Other men uncovered ropes and winches, and ducked beneath walls of spray washing over the ship.

Only when the whaler turned, following the pod, did the bull become really worried. He allowed his cows and calves to overtake him, and urged them on. Now he was between the ship and his pod.

In a straight line, due south, they raced, the hunter and the hunted. The whales spouted more and more frequently as the calves tired, and their mothers nudged them on, frightened by the bull's urgent calls. The noise of the narrow steel bows slamming into the waves grew louder, and the screw noise changed in pitch, terrifying in its intensity. The sonar focussed on the pod, repeating its ominous call monotonously: ping; ping; ping.

No more than twenty yards separated the gunner from the bull, and the man crouched behind his shield, waiting to fire. Closer, and the bull whale moved across the sights. The bows dipped into a trough and then up, high above the bull, whose head rose above a wave. The gunner caught a brief smell of the whale's breath on the wind: the sights held steady, and his finger squeezed the trigger. There was a loud thud, and the ship jolted. Through a cloud of blue smoke the gunner watched orange rope snake a parabola towards the bull's dark shape.

One moment there was the bull's dominant voice

117

urging them on, and then there was a thud and a scream. Nothing, for this pod, was ever to be the same again. The cows turned, and there, twisting in the waves, blood streaming from his back, was their bull, orange rope wrapping around him, as he bucked and rolled in the pink sea. They could not possibly have known what was happening: could not have guessed that this was just the beginning, for they both turned and swam to their master, and called to him: pleading voices asking what they must do. They ignored the steel shadow behind the bull, and the cold bulk of the whaler's bows moving above them. Already the gun was being reloaded, and winches turned, tightening the rope, pulling open barbs deep in the bull's guts. An explosive harpoon might have been more merciful, shocking the whale into instant submission, but these weapons were reserved for the great baleen whales: small whales could be tamed, in the end, with barbed spears.

He struggled for half an hour, diving down beneath the whaler, crying out for help, screaming in fear and agony. The rope tightened and the winches strained, as the barbs cut deeper into his flesh. The cows and calves followed, calling insistently, the urgency in their voices begging him to lead them away to a silent ocean.

At last he wallowed uselessly alongside the whaler's hull. He whimpered to his family, knowing that he was finished, even as ropes and chains passed over him, lashing him against the steel. They wanted to leave, to swim off into the safe quiet ocean, but they were held to that dreadful place by a bond stronger even than the terror they felt. That bond to their bull was to mean more death, more fear and blind blood-gushing agony, for now it was the turn of the cows.

It was an easy shot, difficult only in choice, for there were four surfaced targets for the gunner's aim. He chose the biggest cow, and sent a harpoon into her neck. Her scream shook the whole pod. Even the dying bull gave a weak kick and cried out. She dived, feeling the barbs dig into her spine. She descended two hundred feet, followed all the way by the other cow and the two calves, until the straining winches held her, and turned her up. Above her she saw the whaler's hull, and alongside the bull, encircled by blood. Not knowing why, she kicked away the last of her strength, and head-crashed into the ship's keel. The unyielding steel killed her, mercifully, and she was lashed behind her mate.

The remaining cow called, but no answers came from the two bodies. All she heard was the cold clanking and thudding of steel. She bolted with the two calves, heedless of direction, conscious only that she must take the calves away: anywhere.

Once again the whaler's screws bit into the water, and hearing the whining note, and the increasing throb of the engine, the cow screamed. Instinctively she turned away from the ship's present course, and as the bull had done, she forced the calves to overtake her.

Laden with the extra weight of the two killer whales lashed alongside, the whaler moved slower than before, at not more than twenty knots. Initially the three whales swam much faster, and they had put a mile of ocean between themselves and the enemy before the little calf tired, and slowed almost to a halt.

The whaler drew closer again, inexorably closing the gap, while the cow forced the gasping calf along, calling urgently, encouraging her to speed up.

It was too late: the gunner shot the adult whale. For the

third time the calves saw the spurting blood and the orange rope. They heard the agonised scream, that meant more swimming and diving, more drawn-out moments of terror.

The cow thrashed on the surface, the rope wrapping around her and digging into her flesh. The calves lifted their fore-flippers over her back and tried to pull her down into the sea, but she could not feel or understand them. She just felt the choking sting of salt water entering her lungs, and a fierce pain in her side.

The gun loaders looked questioningly at the gunner. He turned and looked towards the bridge. The captain shook his head. The calves were spared: too small to be worth shooting. The men deserted the gun deck to the music of straining winches, and to the sight of whales' tails lashing the face of a crimson sea.

On an ocean that stank of violence and death the calves were left alone. In two hours their world had changed, irreversibly, from a playground among the waves, to a world of virtual emptiness.

Long after the screw noises were lost in the rustle of the waves the calves called out for their parents. They could not understand that they were calling in vain to dead ears, that they were never again to hear the comforting replies of the adults.

They remained in the same place on the sea for many days. While the blood diffused away, and with it the last taste, the last presence, of their parents, the female calf sank into a state of shock, her amber eyes fading to a lifeless pall. The bull calf remained alert, listening for the noises that could mean a repeat of those two hours of slaughter. Even in his sleep he heard the long submarine screams, the gun explosions, the thudding and clanking

and high-revving engines. Always he woke to the empty
sea, with his sister's body bumping into his in the silence
of the troughs. Somewhere in the oceans of the world the
same slaughter was happening: in Antarctica a finback
screamed out, or a sperm whale crossing the equator felt
the sudden agony cut through his spine; or it could be
another killer whale off Norway's coast, shot while
playing in the whaler's own bow wave. To the young
bull, drifting on the quiet tide, it would always be his
parents, time and time again.

When at last the bull realised the adult whales were not
going to return he called to his sister, and led her south,
away from Iceland. They swam into the running hills of
water, climbing up the steep slopes and blowing, poised
high above the valleys, and then dropping and disappear-
ing through the next wave.

The cow calf had been totally dependent on her
mother's milk. Now cut off from her supply she rapidly
lost condition. The bull knew how to hunt, in a clumsy
sort of way, but the female did not understand what to do
with the fish and cuttlefish that he brought her from the
mid-deeps.

A warm swell lifted by a slow westerly washed over
their backs. The young calf chose that day, while the sun
shone overhead, and the North Atlantic drift carried
them along, and that place, two hundred miles from
Scotland, in which to die. She emitted just one burst of
sound, her first and last since the day of the whaler, a
weak sob, and then the dull light in her eyes was gone.

A raft of puffins, disturbed by the harsh sound of a
whale blow, lifted above the waves. They flew in a wide
circle, watching the two dark shapes beneath them. Then
the larger whale vanished, and the female drifted alone

121

on the tide.

Without stopping, the bull swam towards the sound of far off surf. Two dawns later Cape Wrath, bathed yellow in the sun-rise, met him, and he rested, lulled by the sound of the waves booming and crashing against the Cape's rocks.

Presently he began to call. He had lost all he knew and loved, but the indomitable spirit of life still surged through him; so he called like all the other lonely members of his kind: a plea to be heard far away across the sea, a call of hope. He did not know then that he would have so little time to wait, that friends were so near, and so the sounds he emitted were harrowing and desperate.

Sabre and his family floated on idyllic seas amongst the Hebridean Isles, blissfully unaware of the events that had taken place elsewhere. There might be a day when their own bubble of contentment would break but in the meantime they hunted and played, and slept amongst the island peace: a gift from Nature: beneath the sun.

Chasing mackerel along a swollen tide-rip in the shallows, the three killer whales sped towards Cape Wrath. Sabre, ever wary of the sounds and echoes in the ocean, was the first to hear the bull's voice. Alert, he dived and swam along the floor, watching his mirrored ceiling as he closed on the sound source. Seeing the white belly, shining in the morning light, he rose in front of the young bull in a flurry of foam and spray.

The bewildered bull calf stared at the huge whale surfaced before him. He was silent while the effervescing bubbles cleared, and Sabre's blow drowned the sound of the waves. Two more shapes materialised behind Sabre: Spraylash, a broad smiling-faced cow, and Glowchin, a calf like his sister, though fatter and with wide white markings.

So they found him in the entrance to the North Minch, beneath Cape Wrath. He swam with them over the peaceful seas towards Lewis in the west. Certainly the young bull felt relief. Perhaps he even felt the beginnings of a new happiness welling out of the empty void within him; a new future with these big warm whales.

Four shadows swept across the heaving face of the North Minch. The leader's tall fin cut, sword-like, above the crests. The big female behind him was flanked by two smaller shapes: Glowchin on one side, and on the other the new bull calf: Minch.

In the sea lochs and channels of the Outer Hebrides Minch slipped out of his nightmares, though in his sleep he twitched, and the noise of fishing boats alerted him and made him cry out. He was always awake with the dawn, watching and listening: waiting. But the island summer was soothing, and no high speed propellers hurled sleek snarling hunters into the lochs. The wooden fishing vessels, tubby and slow, offered no threat and never came close. An occasional sailing yacht, pulled by ballooning spinnakers, sliced a foaming wake across the bays. Huge basking sharks ploughed through the surface plankton, and once they saw a fin-back whale off North Uist. But no other large objects disturbed the young bull, and so gradually he became more at peace.

Glowchin drew her new friend into play. With her impatient spirit it did not take long. Teasingly she thumped into his side, and nipped his tail, until he chased her through the waves and down into the stillness of the twilight. To the west of the islands the seas quickly became steep. Here they rolled together down the cascades of the swell, plunging hard into the valleys and hiding there. Or they sneaked up on each other in the body of a climbing wave. Glowchin would thrust right up into the white foam at the summit, and then fall onto Minch's back, feeling him buck for the few seconds before he threw her off. At high tide near the coast they hid from each other in the reefs, and they played ambush by the shallow water wrecks. They learnt to hunt each other, and they learnt to hunt together. Faster than two dolphins they skated across the rollers in pursuit of mackerel. In the sand-bedded estuaries they snatched fleet-finned salmon, and in the blue water far from shore they found sharks.

At night they were at peace together, sleeping side by side, or watching the stars and the moon flashing off the walls of the waves. Spraylash slept with them while the big bull slumbered, or swam slowly around, listening to the sounds of the night.

At first light Minch and Sabre would swim off together, and push their heads through the waves into the early morning spray. They would wait for the breeze to build and rock Spraylash and Glowchin out of sleep. Then the hunting could begin, and after they had filled their bellies the games would start, unless a summer gale sent them hurrying for shelter in the lee of an island.

The idyllic summer slowly burnt itself out. Heavy autumn storms lifted the seas, and made them uncomfortable close to land. Sabre led his pod away from shore into the deep water, and turned them south. They made slow progress with the North Atlantic drift and south westerlies pushing into their faces, but the long processions of surf-veined rollers were an endless playground for the two young whales, and porpoises, also fleeing south with the end of summer, fell across their paths, and provided enough food for their journey.

Far beyond the Continental Shelf they drifted. Other than the animals they hunted, they met with few travellers. A submarine appeared one afternoon. Creeping silently eastward, it crossed their paths at a depth of fifty feet. Coloured in NATO grey, its nuclear engine drove the weapon on its mission. Sinister, it stole across the ocean, submerged for weeks at a time, searching, listening, hunting for enemy vessels, and hiding from mistrustful eyes on the surface. Without once seeing the light of day, the submarine could travel around the world, and only the creatures of the sea would know of its passing. The killer whales heard its approach as it moved through the twilight at slow revolutions, and Sabre swam down to investigate. Ghostlike it loomed out of the haze. Electronic senses knew of the whale's presence, and cameras turned to watch him. A floodlight's beam lanced towards the killer whale, and followed him when he kicked towards the stern. The light blinded Sabre, and the vessel's silent thrust confused him, so he returned to his mystified family at the surface, and allowed the submarine an unhindered passage.

To Sabre the submarine was a hard grey object, bigger than a blue whale, that sent out a continuous pulse of sonar, and drove itself quietly, peacefully, through the gloom. To mankind it was the ultimate weapon. Hidden, even from the electronic eyes of orbiting satellites, it could approach any coast in the world to within striking range of the cities of any nation. Once there it could sit on the ocean floor, at depths of two hundred feet to over a mile; and it could wait. The submarine's nuclear heart supplied its energy and, if necessary, the crew could be kept alive and safe for a year, without the vessel once having to surface for air. It was a self-sufficient unit that could, if the orders came, send a dozen missiles, each armed with an atomic bomb, to obliterate an army, turn cities into radioactive rubble, and cripple a continent: and there, on the sea's floor, the submarine's crew would not even feel the bang. To Sabre it was just a hard grey object bigger than a blue whale.

The killers did not meet another vessel until they were much farther south, five hundred miles west of Portugal. The ocean was a great deal warmer here so close to the tropics, but there were many storms ripping suddenly over the horizon. Rains hammered, monsoon-like, at the waves, and lightning arced between sky and sea. The gusting wind took the storms away towards the Bay of Biscay, and left the seas heaving in their wake.

One night a super-tanker was caught by the hurricane winds. She had been plodding sedately across a smooth ocean, from Africa towards oil-hungry Europe. She carried thousands of tons of crude hydrocarbons, and lay low in the water, while the swell washed across her long decks. The storm crashed into her stern and lifted her propellers out of the waves. Something in the engine room snapped and a boiler blew up, the screws stopped turning, and the crippled super-tanker turned broadside to the waves. Incredibly slowly she climbed each swell. Half her great length was suspended in the air while she passed, creaking and groaning, through the waves. Mountains of water smashed down upon her, and under the stress her external hull began to break. The middle storage hold cracked open and oil gushed into the sea. Then the storm passed, and for the moment the tanker's life was spared, but she spewed ton after ton of oil as she wallowed uselessly in the swell.

Dawn's eager light revealed the night's tragedy. A three mile slick stretched, black and stinking, from the tanker towards the north-east. With luck the engines could be repaired, and the tanker might escape before another storm struck. With luck none of the four remaining holds would be breached. But the hydrocarbons would gush from her middle hold until it was empty, and the slick would grow bigger and ride off towards the shores of Spain. The black tide would clog the coastline, advancing up the yellow sands, leaving carcasses of sea-birds and seals, fish and whales, hanging in the slick; thousands of them.

Slowly the oil would be degraded and broken up. The action of the waves and bacteria would work away ceaselessly, and detergents, themselves poisonous, would be sprayed upon the slick by a hundred boats; but it would be much too late: the black tide would wash against the beaches of Spain, bringing death wherever it touched.

If the tanker was not lucky, if another storm bore down upon her before the engines were ready, or before the oil could be transferred to another ship, the disaster would be much worse.

That very same dawn the killer whales approached the crippled giant. Drifting helplessly, broadside to the seas, she lay across their path. Long before they saw her they tasted the acrid pungency of the oil, and soon the surface above them was dashed with black streaks. As the taste grew more intense they turned and swam up-wind, parallel to the slick. Then the supertanker's bulk, decks awash with oil and water, loomed in front of them, and her great malignant presence, together with the stench of death, frightened them. Quickly they passed by the wounded ship and left the bitter taste behind. The killer whales had missed the main part of the slick: they had been lucky. Many would not be so lucky.

They moved across a warm tumbling seascape, basking in the sun, drifting, playing on the swollen hills, and diving far into the deep. A few migrants saw them pass: a tern skipped and dipped across the crests, and settled for a brief moment upon Spraylash's exposed back. A lonely boar dolphin came face to face with Glowchin in the trough of a deep swell. His blue and white shape streaked off into the sea, before the killer whales could find his echo amongst the pitching waves. One night they heard the voice of a humpback whale a long way off, but by morning this too was lost amongst the remote cubic miles of the ocean. A few of the sea's nomads they caught; seals, sharks, and once a turtle, whose shell was smashed between Sabre's jaws as if it were the skin of a mackerel rather than the hard armour of this marine reptile.

The air they breathed became hotter, and the sea was smooth and glassy. For weeks they continued to move south, and presently they crossed the Tropic of Cancer. The coast of Africa lay five hundred miles to the east, and to their south were the Cape Verde islands shimmering in the heat haze.

Sabre remembered these waters from the time when he had visited them with the Great School. He remembered too the White shark that had destroyed a calf before Forkfin could catch and annihilate the snarling-jawed menace. There were sharks now, always there; somewhere. The sleek shapes would circle the killer whales, gradually sneaking closer, waiting for a chance to strike.

They would appear on the edge of Sabre's sonar range and move in, sometimes gingerly, sometimes swiftly, with their maniac purpose. In the clear water the whales would see the grey torpedoes slide out of the distance, mean eyes glowing with hunger. Sabre and Minch swam far faster than the sharks, who could not turn quickly enough to escape as the killers swept up into their soft bellies like submarine battering-rams. But the big bull whale paid careful attention to each new attacker, for he knew giants swam out there that could hurtle in and tear Glowchin in two, if he was not fast enough to intercept. Even Spraylash would not be able to fight a forty foot Great White, so Sabre listened to the shapes that hovered and circled beyond the limits of vision.

Abruptly they came into shallow water above sun patterned island shoals. Multi-hued corals clothed the rocks, and brilliantly coloured fish bobbed and darted amongst the calcerous pinnacles. Anemones, red, vermilion and purple, sat in advantageous positions upon the reefs, and fields of kelp swayed in the tide. Jelly fish and Portuguese Men of War floated on the surface, trailing their long venomous tendrils wafting about in search of prey.

The smell of an island's shore scented the air, with the predominant odour of weed and fish rotting on the beach beneath a tropical sun. Sounds, different from those of the open ocean, crept across the bays: long white breakers rumbling up the coast; men, sweating and swearing, repairing old wooden boats; the warm breeze rustling through palms; crabs and creatures of the sandy floor going about their scavenging, throwing up little yellow clouds that hung and twinkled briefly in the sunlight before resettling to the contours of the bed. Character again after the long swim across the void of the deep sea.

In a shallow channel dividing two islands Sabre heard two echoes to his sonar. His hunter's brain quickened, and he dropped down to the sandy floor and kicked smoothly towards the targets.

Suspended in the sea above him were two men, each wearing an air tank. They were treasure hunters, looking for signs of Spanish galleons that had sunk in these waters. Several gold-laden vessels from Africa and the Americas had sought sanctuary from storms amongst the Cape Verde islands, only to stumble upon reefs and shoals. Now the two men hunted for the priceless cargoes of the ships that had been wrecks for hundreds of years.

Sabre saw the two men and the clouds of silver bubbles streaming from their masks. Slowly he lifted himself towards them. Simultaneously they saw the huge killer whale rising beneath them. Terror must have flashed through their minds, and one of them spat out his air-piece in panic, but their occupation had brought them close to death many times. They had met several species of shark, and worse, they had been too close to big conger eels, or quick-jawed morays that skulked about the wrecks, but never had they been so close to something so vast as a big killer whale. In a moment Sabre moved between them and continued towards the surface. They felt the tremendous wash of water tumble them over, and when they re-orientated, the shadow of the whale was passing over them. They looked up and saw the great white underside. Sabre twisted, with incredible grace for his bulk, and came face to face with the divers.

Members of the two most intelligent species on earth stared at one another. Close together in space, kept worlds apart by environment and understanding.

Life had begun in the sea. Taking millions of years to
evolve, animals had crawled and slid away from the
waters of their birth and had begun to colonise the land.
Still evolution carried on, producing many diverse species. Some became successful on land, others were called
back to the sea. About a hundred million years ago, long
before the dinosaurs became extinct, a species of mammal that was eventually to give rise to *Cetacea*, the
whales, had returned to the shallow waters, while other
mammals remained on land and forgot about the sea.
Some were successful, while others adapted to become so.

Evolution's most stunning examples now stared at
each other across the genetic millennia that separated
them. The humans, with hearts pounding in their chests,
hung motionless, hardly daring to breathe, terrified. The
killer whale, also motionless, could not have been scared
for this was his own environment, but these were strange
creatures, small, ungainly, and he could sense their fear:
yet there was something more, something totally
beyond his understanding, but something ...

Sabre may not consciously have known why he left the
gangly-limbed creatures unharmed. Perhaps he forgot
them even as he turned away, brushing gently past them
as he moved off towards Glowchin's calls; but there may
have been more understanding of the encounter in the
killer whale's mind than in the minds of the men, who
rushed towards the safety of their boat as soon as the
whale's shape merged into the haze. And it is more than
likely that neither creature, whale nor man, understood
anything about the other, for the millions of years that
divided them formed a deep dark gorge that may never
be lit.

Whaler

TWIN-SCREWED IT SPED, fiercely, across the ocean. All across the wide North Atlantic it hunted, from the equator to the Arctic wastes, from Baffin Bay off the Canadian coast to the Barents Sea of Northern Russia. It had shot Right whales beneath the towering black pinnacles of Bear Island, killer whales off Iceland and Norway, fin-backs off the coast of Africa, and humpbacks down the eastern United States and into the Caribbean. On the open ocean it had taken blues and rorquals, sperms and seis, bottle-nosed whales and pilots. It had taken them all, and many. The ship was a Russian, sleek, high-bowed and fast. It was capable of swallowing five hundred tons of whale meat before returning to the mother ship, the factory, which plodded its laden way across the migration lines of the great whales. Hungry Russia waited while her killers plundered the last remnants of the Cetacean species. The factory waited while her catchers roamed the seas just beyond the horizon. Most days there was nothing, but then, in the distance, a puff of vapour shone above the rolling hills of water, and immediately the screws bit into the sea.

A fin-back and a humpback swam together towards the sound and taste of the sun-baked Azores. The strange couple had been together for over a year, keeping each other company in the lonely blue reaches of the Atlantic.

They had both lost their schools to the whalers, and neither had found any other whales of its own type. But they had found each other, and though their songs were different they were whales, and each understood instinctively a little of the ways of the other; and passing the months with a friend was much better than being alone. Mouths agape they rolled towards the islands through the cloudy plankton soup. Their mouths closed and the huge tongues moved across long arching baleen plates. Between them at this time of the year, when the food was there, six tons of plankton were harvested every day.

The humpback was noisier than the fin. He gushed out wide streams of bubbles, and smashed his long flippers and flukes on the surface of calm seas. Sometimes he jumped to remove parasites that irritated his tough hide. Often he jumped for fun, and his whole floppy forty feet hung above white curtains of spray. His song was louder than the fin's, the notes reaching far into the ocean's distance, but he had heard no reply from other humpbacks for over two years. The fin, though a less intelligent animal, was longer and faster than the humpback, and sometimes he was frustrated by his friend's lazy progress, for he belonged to a species of whale that could cross an ocean in a month. But he did not leave his dark friend because it seemed there was nowhere in particular to go, no voices calling him away; and the humpback could always find plankton ... Two friends, together, yet alone on a sky-swept sea.

It was the humpback's boisterous blow that first attracted the keen eyes of the Russian sighter. Engines revved, and the steel killer turned towards its targets, throwing a long curving wake as it charged over the smooth surface.

This once, this precious once, there was another visitor to the Azores: a conservation ship, an ex-trawler, slow, out-dated and old, she had plodded, expensively, from the Thames' estuary out into the whaling arenas of the North Atlantic. She was British, and represented the country that, ironically, had shown the world the fat profits to be made out of commercial whaling; but which now, along with America and some others, acted as a conscience to the rest of the world, and tried, desperately, to stop the slaughter of the last of the whales. Her name was *Gladiator*, and she had been at sea for three months with very little success in her quest. She was too slow, too small, and too old. Now she chugged towards the Azores for refuelling and repairs.

Gladiator's crew were as unlikely as the ship. Mostly young men they came from all walks of life. Most were there because they felt strongly about what was happening to the whales and what the slaughter meant in our 'enlightened' age, and this was their way of doing something positive for their cause. A few were there just for the hell of it. Some were wealthy, others had nothing but their strong belief in what they were trying to do. Some were sailors; most were not. All on board *Gladiator* were there for one end: to stop the whalers.

In the three months since *Gladiator* had left the Thames' estuary she had not managed to 'save' a single whale, though her crew had filmed the slaughter time and time again, and hoped to show the films, via the media, to the largest international audience possible. In this way at least they could gain support and some finance: so diesel fuel and food awaited them in the Azores.

The bridge crew of *Gladiator* saw the two whales and the Russian whaler simultaneously. Perhaps this time luck was with them. The whales were close, and the Russian still a fair way off: there was time.

Gladiator stopped, and two rubber boats were lowered over the side. Men climbed into them, three in each, and big out-board motors spluttered into life. They were off, hurtling across the smooth sea towards the whales.

In the sudden loud commotion of propeller noises, the distant twin screws of the whaler, *Gladiator*'s heavy thudding and the whining out-board motors, the whales dived, the humpback's big white flukes waving good-bye above a whirlpool, as the huge beasts submerged. But it was not going to be as easy as that.

The rubber boats waited on the billowing water while the whaler cut towards them, with its big curling bow-wave dazzling in the sun. Men gazed anxiously across the blue sea. The Azores shimmered like a mirage on the horizon, *Gladiator* plodded on towards the small boats, and the whaler lanced ahead of a thin trail of smoke and a stark line of white foam. Then, two hundred yards from where they had last seen them, the whales surfaced, and two loud blows shook the still air. Again the humpback's tail lifted slowly, almost nonchalantly, into the air. Hungry eyes aboard the whaler, and concerned eyes on the rubber boats watched the speckled tail drop smoothly into the swell as the big whale dived again.

The conservationists moved off in the direction of the whales while the Russian thundered in pursuit, closing, rapidly, the gap that separated the whales from safety. They could hear her now, a screaming high-torque engine racing at full speed, and water hissing and crashing in the ship's path. Shapes were seen moving on the decks,

135

and one shape stood ominously behind the big harpoon cannon high in the bows. The men in the boats waited, nerves tensed, for the conflict that was soon to begin, the conflict that in the past had so often gone wrong, when they had arrived too late to do anything more than film the whole sequence of events, from the flying harpoon to the flensing knives glinting in the sunlight as the whale was finally torn apart. But this time at least they were not too late, and with spirit and determination they might be able to prevent the harpoons from flying.

The conservationists were less than a hundred feet from the whales now and could see their bodies in the clear blue water. The humpback was stocky and rounded, with long pale flippers and flukes. Many calcerous growths and nodules marked his dark hide. The fin-back looked the part of his ocean-going breed: a long, stream-lined, blue-grey shape, seemingly poised for an instant burst of power. Between them they were worth some forty thousand pounds: two friends, side by side.

Both whales were now frightened. Memories of days years ago, when whalers had found their schools, made them drive their great flukes, so that trembling ridges of water formed above them. The fin-back thrust ahead, picking up quickly to a speed of over thirty miles an hour. The humpback forced himself on in his friend's slipstream, but he belonged to a species that was not built for high velocity travel. The finback could swim at his present rate for an hour, and not surface to blow once in all that time, while his friend, striving in his wake, would have to blow more and more frequently under any sustained stress. For the time being they both surged on as the whining notes of propellers filled the sea.

Revved down to one-third speed the Russian loomed,

enormous, above the two rubber boats. The immobile face of the gunner looked down at the conservationists. The confrontation had begun. While the boats stayed between the whales and the whaler it was risky firing a harpoon: the grenaded head could blow a man to nothing, and the lashing tail of a harpooned whale could destroy a small boat, and all lives in it, with one single sweep. So for an hour, on that hot afternoon, the position remained a stalemate: two whales, two rubber boats, and the big deadly shape of the whaler; and a mile astern of that was *Gladiator*: a straight line of conflict reaching towards the Azores.

The gunner had left his position soon after the meeting and had gone to the bridge. Now he returned, set-faced, to his cannon. The engine slipped into higher revs and the whaler began to zig-zag from side to side. The gunner stared along his sights, and moved the cannon so that the fleeting shapes of the whales were always in his view. But too often a human head or a black rubber boat crossed his sights, so his finger remained stationary above the trigger.

The Russian's helmsman took the vessel out to the side, and suddenly the screws lurched into full power in an attempt to overtake the conservationists, giving the gunner a clear shot at a whale; but one of the boats responded, and moved to obscure the line of fire. For another hour the whaler tried to slip around the rubber boats for a clear aim, but each attempt was foiled. In the end, partly out of frustration, partly in anger, the gunner squeezed the trigger, as the humpback's dark head rose into the air. It was a long shot, and a poor one. The conservationists heard the explosion almost directly overhead, and were showered with the hot ash of the detonator. Immediately they saw the white rope snaking above them, and the cloud of blue smoke. Then they saw the splash just beyond the fin-back. The harpoon had missed both whales, passing above them, and falling harmlessly into the sea. A series of oaths escaped from the Russian's decks: the gunner remained impassive, and signalled for his cannon to be reloaded.

The fin-back felt the rope slide along his back. In panic he rose to the surface for a quick spout, and then bolted, calling for his friend to follow; but the humpback was tired after the hours of hard swimming and could not speed up. Now he was frightened and silent. He swam until his whole colossal body ached, and he longed to be rid of the savage noises behind him. He wanted only to be swimming with the fin-back through quiet blooms of plankton in the sun-dappled waters of the islands.

Fearing the whaler would now use its speed to pursue the fin-back, one of the boats sped after the fleeing whale, while the other remained with the humpback. The Russian stayed with the smaller whale, for though a lower weight, a humpback yields more oil than a fin-back and is more valuable. Also, when panicked, the latter species is a lot more difficult to catch.

The humpback wallowed on the surface, the smell of his breath thick in the air. Now and then one of his long noduled flippers splashed into the air in a gesture of defeat, and his great tired body would roll into the blue; but, within seconds, the water bulged and his head would breach the sea.

The Russian circled its target, twisting and yawing like a destroyer hunting down a submarine; but each time the gunner held the humpback in his sights his protectors hurtled into view, and the chance was gone.

Gladiator chugged on to the scene. Men's voices, amplified harshly by megaphones, traversed the space between the two ships: angry voices, Russian and English voices; two peoples close together in space, kept worlds apart by man-made barriers.

The exchange of words ended as dusk was falling. The sea and the sky darkened, and the humpback could be seen only when he broke the surface. The gunner no longer had a shadow to aim at. The position became more hopeful for the whale, and more urgent for the Russian. Another shot, sounding more intense than the first in the stillness of gathering dusk, rang out, and all eyes watched the brief parabolic travel of the heavy harpoon. The gunner had aimed at a bulge in the water a second before he realised his mistake. The whale had turned, and beneath the bulge there were only his lifting flukes. The harpoon nicked the edge of his tail, and then shot on uselessly into the sea. A sting of pain caused the humpback to leap half clear of the surface. Yards only from the rubber boat he reared up, a dark colossus of the deep, and fell thunderously towards his protectors. A wall of water swept over them, and they were all thrown into the sea.

The conservationists survived. They crawled, winded and stunned, back into the boat. They limped towards *Gladiator*, while the other rubber boat whined back across the dusk-lit sea towards the scene. The fin-back was now miles away and safe; the humpback wallowed on the far side of *Gladiator*. In the shock of activity the Russian stopped engines, and rocked quietly in the gentle swell. The Azores and the contesting ships faded serenely into a tropical twilight.

Navigation lights winked on board the ships. Today the whaler was beaten: two harpoons spent for no reward, two oil-rich prizes snatched from the Russians' grasp; two friends who tomorrow would find each other in the shadow of an island, and could swim unharassed through plankton-clouded shallows. This once the team work, the effort and the courage had all worked: two whales had been given another chance. There was much celebration aboard *Gladiator* that night, and new heart in their mission. The Russian stole off to the west, a fresh anger throbbing in her roaring engines, and a new grim determination within her crew. She thrust out her gleaming bow-wave like a tiger with a white bone in its teeth, an irridescent line marking her swift passage towards the horizon. Tomorrow the cannon would be reloaded; the next time they saw whales there would be no Englishmen in the way.

The humpback found his friend at dawn. Neither whale was any the worse for his experience, save for a small notch in the humpback's tail. They lazed away the day, lulled by the island peace: two friends, together beneath a tropical sun.

For days the killer whales drifted around the islands' shallows or across the deep blue sounds and channels. The warm seas and the long days of the sun-drenched Azores had taken the edge off their appetites. They killed little, and drifted aimlessly with the tide. Minch and Glowchin played their games of tag, and chased fish amongst the weed-clothed reefs and corals. Fishermen watched anxiously as Sabre led his pod from island to island, his big black fin stark and threatening as it lanced above the tilting seas. But they had no need to fear, for there was no menace in the killer whales' presence amongst the islands. They had arrived from the featureless open Atlantic, the running hills of water of an apparently endless ocean. Here there was refuge from the days and nights of monotonous swimming and hunting. The islands afforded shelter, and peace, and character, after the millions of cubic miles of emptiness.

There was little in the sea to cause them alarm. Minch was slightly wary of the fishing boats, as the old vessels plodded above the time-proven fishing grounds. In the deep water the whales met with huge white liners, cutting slowly and majestically along passenger-designed routes, towards the yellow beaches and luxury hotels of the Azores.

A big White shark appeared one dawn, and cast a mean gaze over Glowchin's plump body; but even as Sabre and Minch turned towards the beast, it flicked its vast tail and shot off into the gloom. The killer whales listened to its echo as the shark sped off into the deep sea, and then they forgot about it. With a new day breaking there could be games or quiet slumber on the surface. The White shark would not return, and in the food-rich island seas there was no need to chase sharks through the deep.

Had Sabre and Minch pursued the shark the whaler might never have sighted the killer whales. As it happened Sabre's tall spout just caught the quick Russian eyes, while the noon sun beat down upon a subdued ocean. The sighter could not be sure: the surface danced and waved about in the heat haze, but, silhouetted against the nearest island lying ten miles to the east, he saw the white shimmering blow. Within two minutes the ship turned, and her engine revolutions increased. Men swept over the decks, pulling at covers, and preparing winches and ropes. Three men moved towards the cannon carrying the dark shape of an armed harpoon. This time there were no Englishmen on the heat-warped horizon.

Minch was the first to hear it. He cried out suddenly and fearfully, for he had heard that note before. Then Sabre heard the screw noise as it hummed and whined above the ocean sounds. It was still a long way off, and seemingly no more threatening than the other ships they had met in the Azores. Minch cried out again, focussing the sound towards Sabre: an urgent call. Then the young bull thrust towards Glowchin and pushed hard into her flank, and called for her to swim: swim hard towards the islands. Spraylash and Glowchin did not understand Minch's sudden change of behaviour, but something in Sabre's brain responded to those pleading, distressed calls, and he made his decision. The leader roared his command, and turned, as Minch urged, towards the island in the east. They blew as one, and then thrust themselves down thirty feet into the sea, where they accelerated through the sun-dappled waters towards the far away sound of breaking waves.

The Russian's twin screws spun at maximum revolutions, and a great shining veil of spray arced away from her bows. The gunner stood, expectant, on the cannon platform, feeling the blast of humid tropical air rush by as the whaler picked up to full speed.

If it had not been for Minch's advance warning and instant alarm; for Sabre's quick command, and the driving blast of power from each of the four whales, the Russian would even now be bearing down on them, and a dark back would be held in the gunner's sights for the brief seconds he needed to squeeze the trigger. But they had had the warning, and killer whales are exceptionally fast swimmers, faster even than a fin-back or the smaller dolphins.

They had to blow. Synchronously they rose, levelled off, cartwheeled, blew and dived, all in one beautifully executed manoeuvre, which left barely a mark on the surface. Their flukes swept them on. Now it was easy: now they were fresh, and their high speed flight was just a burst of energy such as they might use during a hunt. But the Russian was a vessel designed to chase and catch fast-moving whales. Faster than a Second World War destroyer, its engines could maintain the power blast until the fastest creatures in the sea were exhausted and spent. The gap between the killer whales and the whaler closed.

Sabre was in the lead, and his body created a wide slipstream in which Spraylash and Glowchin could swim, while Minch followed closely behind also taking advantage of the lower resistance in the wake of the big whales. It was Minch who first noticed the increased intensity of the whaler's propellers, and it was his terror-filled voice which forced Sabre to become really worried.

Foreflippers thrust out, angles changed, and the four shadows ascended into the intense tropical light. They blew and were gone, but many eyes aboard the whaler saw their quick shining spout, and the gunner's keen eyes caught a glimpse of Sabre's tall dorsal fin. This was the place to be: high in the bows of the fastest ship in the Atlantic fleet, with the engines racing, the winches and ropes all ready, and a heavy, high-charge harpoon in his cannon, the salt kiss of the ocean in his face, a wild feeling welling within, and a big bull killer whale his target.

Glowchin was the first to tire. She rose and broke

143

clumsily above the swell. She did not roll down immediately but spouted three times. The Russian's engines hammered out their note, and now the hissing of their bow-wave could be heard. Minch and Sabre nudged into Glowchin, spurring her on, but she could not maintain that initial surge, and the island shallows were too far away, the crashing steel noises too close.

Perhaps it was instinct, or possibly some calculated thought, that made Sabre do it. He called out to his three wards to continue towards the island. Then he left them and thrust out into the sea, but his voice and command remained with them as Spraylash now led the way towards safety. He had to give them time; time to reach the shallows. He blew aggressively, exposing half his body broadside to the whaler. They saw him and started to turn, to follow the ridged paths formed by his great sweeping tail on the surface.

It is an old whaler's trick not to give chase to a dominant bull that is acting as decoy for his school, drawing a whaler's attention. If the cows are pursued the bull always returns, and presents his tired wide flank as he tries to protect the others. So the Russian swerved as the enticing tall fin rose flashing above the sea, but then the ship corrected its course and sped on to follow the slower-moving shapes sliding towards the island.

Sabre had swum four hundred yards before he noticed the dying pitch of the whaler's voice. Half a mile now separated him from Spraylash and the others, and the whaler, which should have been closing on him, was closer by far to his pod. He braked and twisted upwards, so that his head turned above the waves and he could see what was happening towards the island. It was close, very close, but not close enough. They had not reached the shallows and the whaler rushed on still with miles to spare. Sabre heard Minch's scream sweep through the sea. He did not know why the big fast-moving ship meant terror to the young bull; but he could sense the threat it posed with its determined beating voice and its single-minded travel. Spraylash was beneath its bows and he was out here, too far away.

With a roar he plunged down into the sea. Many eyes aboard the whaler were fixed in his direction. They saw his broad head as he breached, and then his cartwheeling back as he lunged himself towards them, the great fin cutting down through the spray. Then for a moment they lost him beneath the turbulence, until the dark shadow appeared hurtling towards them like an enormous black torpedo bent on their destruction. Without blowing once Sabre covered the distance to the Russian, accelerating all the way. As he neared the ship he surfaced and rolled towards the starboard bow. They saw the wide flukes kicking him on, and his fin, taller than a man. Then they felt the shock through the entire ship, from the engine room to the bridge, as the killer whale slammed against the hull. But even a male killer whale travelling at over forty miles an hour can do nothing to a steel hull that can carve a passage through pack-ice. Sabre was pushed aside like a piece of flotsam floating in the sea. Stunned, he rolled on to his side, while the pain in his skull subsided and a fresh anger bit into his heart. The unthinkable was happening: an enemy now lay between himself and Spraylash; an enemy with a roaring voice; an enemy that could not be smashed aside or distracted, one from whom they could not escape, and an enemy that meant terror to Minch, and perhaps the end of everything for them all.

He kicked himself upright and gasped at the humid air, then, turning towards the receding bulk of the ship, he thrust himself in pursuit. Now it was up to him. If he allowed this new terror to destroy his world, to take Spraylash away, and Glowchin and Minch, then why had it all been? Why Seal Island and the Great School, the long months alone, the ice and that first day when he realised he was no longer alone?

There lay the whaler, and beyond that was Spraylash with her calf and Minch, and beyond them there was nothing but water, with the island ahead, much clearer now, but still too far away for safety. Again the crew watched as Sabre closed on them. They were travelling at full speed, but still he caught them; his tail sweeping and driving, his foreflippers held tightly to his chest, his dorsal in the air, and a great wedge of water sliding over his back. He had swum like this many times before, ripping across the face of the deep for sharks and dolphins, but never before had he kicked so hard for so long, with so much determination and fear in his heart. As he swept down the Russian's side he heard Spraylash's voice above the thrashing and slamming of the whaler's engines. She was calling for him, as she and Minch pushed Glowchin across the surface towards the dark mass of the island. Now, when she needed him most, her bull was not at her side. While the sharp V of the whaler's bows cut towards her, Sabre had called to her and sent her away, while his shape diffused into the ocean's gloom. She was frightened, for he had not returned. Glowchin was exhausted and swam slowly, continuously breaching to blow. Minch swam at the calf's side, spurring her on, in the same way he had encouraged his sister in the cold northern waters off Iceland when similar engine noises flooded the sea. But so far there had been no coughing thud rippling across the surface, or ropes snaking into the blue, and no foaming red trails. And no screams.

Then, as the whaler's hull grew above them, they saw Sabre. All eyes, killer whale and human, were turned towards the big bull. The ship's crew crowded against the starboard rail gazing at his awesome shape: hard-bitten whaler-men, impressed by a whale that could swim faster than a fleet catcher travelling at full speed. He had rammed them, and recovered enough to catch up, and then overtake them to reach his pod: Nature's proudest ambassador. No eyes were more impressed than those of the gunner, who saw Sabre's shadow as it swept beneath the cannon-deck. He hugged into the comforting curves of his weapon, for a whaler's reputation depends entirely on his kill rate, that is the number of harpoons expended versus whales killed. The gunner was good and was admired through all the fleet and the ports of home; but yesterday had been bad. Two harpoons fired for no return, and the targets had been big and should not have been missed. The conservationists were merely incidental. Today he was presented with this chance of squaring the record, and bringing smiles back to the faces of the crew, for killer whales, fast and relatively small, are not easy targets compared with big baleen whales, and if he could hit all four whales with the same number of harpoons then the day would be good, and he could forget yesterday's failure: and it would look good back home in Russia.

It would have to be in the next few moments for the island shallows were too close for further delay. The only way to stop the whales was to hit one of them and hold tight with the winches. The bull's back was the obvious target, huge and round, humping above the waves: if only the great angry beast would stop swerving about. It would have to be a good shot, hard into the middle of the back. The rest would be easy: three more shots and the world would smile upon him again. Flensing knives could flash in the evening sunlight, the bitter addictive smell of melting whale fat would hang over the ship while the carcasses were digested; happy radio messages could cross the tropical seas, perhaps all the way back home to Murmansk.

The gunner had been cradling his weapon until his muscles cramped. So often Sabre's back moved across the sights, but then a splash of water, or a tail, or the ship's movement spoilt the shot, and caused the gunner's trigger finger to ease: but there were seconds only before the ship would have to slow or turn.

It was a strain now even for Sabre, but neither he nor Spraylash nor even Minch were finished. Glowchin held them back; she simply could not build up any speed, and wallowed and cried, and gushed high hot spouts, while her father urgently pushed her towards the shallows. Twice she was launched into the air as the big bull flung her out of the path of the whaler's bows.

The whales heard the thud and the hard splash of something hitting the sea close by, and suddenly there was rope everywhere, and a cloud of blood puffed out into the sea. There was a scream; but it was not the cry of a harpooned whale. It was Minch, who remembered these sights and sounds too well.

The gunner stared, dark-eyed, as the smoke cleared and the bows dipped down. There was the white line of rope streaking into the deep. There was the crimson stain and a whale threshing and bucking: but he knew he had missed. There were going to be no smiles from the crew after all, and back home they would all say he was finished. Three harpoons in a row; two yesterday, one today. One miss — well it happened: two and you swore a bit; but three ... It would not look good back in Russia.

Sabre felt the stab of pain a moment after the thud, and then he felt a numbing sting burn into his broadside, but there was no more than that. The harpoon had missed its main target, and had gouged a red trail along his side. He was still alive and in command. And angry.

The few minutes that it took for the cannon to be reloaded was enough. Sabre heard the sound of the ship falling away behind him at the same moment as he saw the hazy yellow of weed-flecked sand beneath him. They had reached the shallows of a wide bay, and the Russian had come as far as she dared. Neither could the whales venture farther. It was dangerous being so close to the sounds of breakers and reef-surf, but at least for the present they were safe from their pursuer.

They gasped at the hot shore-line air, calling quietly, reassuringly, to one another. The ordeal might not be over; the Russian was still there, churning the deep water just beyond the reefs: but it was a reprieve, a rest, and while the tide was still running it was safe enough. Darkness would fall soon, and then they might be able to steal away in the night: away from the islands and the hunters.

Glowchin lay on the surface exhausted with shock. Sabre held her above the waves with an outstretched fore flipper. Spraylash nudged them both, and felt the soothing burn of her relaxing muscles. Her bull had not deserted her after all. In the last moment, it seemed, he had returned to force them to the sands. And so they were all together; almost stranded upon island shoals, an uncomfortable refuge surrounded by beaches and sharp fingers of rock, with coral lancing to the surface. The only escape must in the end lie out there: the safe blue ocean, wide and lonely, featureless acres of pitching swollen hills with foam-dashed crests. Out there beyond the Russians.

It was Minch in the end who took the whaler away across the sea. It could have been the claustrophobia of the shallow water, or just sheer fright; but it could have been something else: for, while the Russian's screws sent out their threatening voice across the mouth of the bay, he seemed to change. He swam quietly round his three friends, brushing gently along their bodies as he passed them by. Suddenly he was not the nervous orphaned bull calf they had found in the Scottish Isles, the bull whom Glowchin had coaxed into play in the dancing crests of summer seas, the Minch who had slumbered fitfully, twitching through the night, awakening and listening for noises of violence and terror seeping from somewhere beyond the ocean's horizon. Now he was none of these things, and when he reached Glowchin, last of all, he slid confidently and purposefully down her flank in a way he had never done before. A quick fire flared up within her that she did not understand, and when she turned towards Minch he was gone.

Sabre's voice cut through the sea. The big bull had realised too late what Minch was doing. Now the young whale had too much distance and speed for Sabre to catch him. The master called to Minch to return, but he knew that he would not be obeyed, and he himself could not leave Spraylash and Glowchin with the whaler so close.

In the gloom of evening the Russian's crew saw him coming. His bow-wave, a high rolling V of flame caught by the setting sun, etched his high speed passage out of the bay. The whaler slewed through one hundred and eighty degrees and lurched in pursuit. They did not know that the fleeing whale was one of the adolescents hardly worth a shot, for beneath the dark surface they could see none of the whale's form. They all imagined that it was the big adult bull, making another decoy dash in a last desperate attempt to draw the whaler away from his pod.

Sabre did not call out again for Minch, nor did Spraylash, and Glowchin could not understand that her playmate had gone. They listened to the screw noises disappear amongst the wave sounds, and then Glowchin cried out plaintively, while darkness fell across their bay.

In the night, while the tide ebbed, they manoeuvred past the reefs and kicked out to sea. Soon the sounds of surf and breakers were left behind, and were replaced with the deep sucking rumble of big rollers. They welcomed the characterless anonymity of the deep water. Here, they would not be able to forget what had happened, but the shock would slowly disperse into the Atlantic's bulk.

A dawn light revealed a hazy tilting world. The killer whales swam slowly, quietly, north. If Minch had been with them they would not have been silent. Glowchin would have seen the waves as hiding places, where she could steal up on Minch, slide mischievously down a slope and try to nip his tail. They could have had play fights and games of tag, and they could have jumped into the air, snapping at clouds and gulls, and felt the hot sting as they hit the sea. The four could have hunted for fish shoals, and they could have turned an acre of the surface into a glistening silver cloud of scales: or they could have sung and been at peace in the early light of the sub-tropics: but Minch was not with them. They did not know where he was, only that he was gone. They could perhaps imagine that the Russian was still chasing him, or that ropes were wrapping around him, restraining him, or that the sharp V of the bows was cutting him in two.

Now Sabre would have to listen even more intently to the noises of the sea, for this sound that had taken Minch away might once again threaten them all. Even the far off murmur of a fishing trawler could not be trusted, or the low thudding of a super-tanker plodding across the horizon. But most of all he would listen for the whine of high speed propellers that suddenly appeared, even before his sensitive sonar had picked up the ship's bulk hurtling its shallow draught through the waves. That noise was the real danger: Minch had taught him that.

The Shores of Home

THERE WAS A crispness to the sea, the cool hard tang of the northern ocean, fast-running swells, crested and fresh, after the long heady rollers of the tropics. In these cold waters appetites sharpened and stomachs gurgled: the killer whales became hunters again. There were more seals here, and porpoises swam amongst the mackerel shoals, and the sinister grey forms of sharks flicked out of the gloom. Sonars clicked and chirped, and echoes told more than any eye could see. Away to the east, Hebridean hills, blue in the early summer light, rose above the sea. Westerly breezes, fickle in temper, lifted the waves, and warmed the surface layers where land-pointed salmon shoals hovered and clustered together for protection from their predators. Rafts of puffins darkened the surface, while gannets and herring gulls dive-bombed the fish shoals. Somewhere to landward a seal barked. Billowing white cumulus drifted across the multi-hued ceiling, and hanging in the focal point of this existence was the late May sun, supplying its energy. To all this the wanderers had returned.

Quickly at first the whales approached the island shoals. Then, as the sounds, tastes and smells of the Hebrides flooded their senses, they slowed down. They were home. A falcon gliding high above the cliffs was the first to notice the three dark shapes travelling towards the green water of the shallows. He screeched and stooped away towards the heather moors, as the killer whales moved across the sands. A stag, drinking from a small burn running into the sea, suddenly caught the smell of a whale's breath on the breeze. Alerted by the carnivorous tang, he lifted his antlered head and sniffed the air. His hooves cluttered on the bare boulders of the stream, as he trod his way towards his herd in the hills. Two juvenile seals lay dozing on the sun-warmed rocks waiting for the tide to reach them. The shock of a whale's blow close by made them stir, and their watery eyes turned towards the sea. Soon they hauled themselves higher above the surf, and settled down for a long afternoon in the sun.

Many eyes did not see the killer whales arrive until it was too late. A huge halibut was caught on the sea bed as he foraged in the silt. A Greak Skua, resting on the sea, was snatched down before his long wings could take a single beat. Gannets diving headlong into the waves in pursuit of small fish caught the attention of the killer whales, and two birds were taken before the remainder knew what was happening. The gannets eventually banked steeply away from the dark shapes beneath them and sped towards the cliffs, leaving their hard-found fish shoals and their two comrades to the whales. Hunger was preferable to death.

The arrival of the killers was a shock to the wildlife of the Scottish Isles; but this was the time of the great harvest, when Nature's banks burst, and life flushed into the temperate seas. The whales were fed and yet the balance remained. The raucous frenzy of the crowded bird colonies still filled the air around the rocks and cliffs. The bounty of May provided for all.

When night came it fell softly, as if to welcome the killer whales home after their ocean ordeal. The western

horizon held the warm glow long after sunset, and a
stillness crept into the air, more like the sultry short
nights of late June than May. Even in the east the mountains were dark against the sky. Beneath the mountains
the deep lochs were still, their surfaces disturbed only by
rising trout, and insects that had lost their way and fallen
into the quiet trap where the fish could mop them up in
the leisure of the night. Moths fluttered in the warm air
and were chased by bats, guided by the high sonar which
criss-crossed the winged mammals' twisting flightpaths.
Young salmon, grilse, surged into the rivers and kicked
their way upstream. Sharp eyed otters saw the silver
flashes above the rapids. They slipped, streamlined, into
the water, and hunted in the glass-smooth pools beneath
the light of a full moon. The sea slept, the tide pushing
weakly against the rocks and nudging up the sands; but
beneath the surface there were many sounds, for without
the crash and rumble of the waves an ear could hear those
noises that were more subtle and delicate than the sea's
powerful voice. Currents whispered through swaying
forests of weeds, shoals of fish hissed in their motion, and
there was the intermittent thud as a predator made a
nocturnal kill. A lobster rasped his claws, and a big crab
clattered noisily on the rocks. Whale and dolphin sonar,
the subtlest and strangest noises of all, formed a cob-
web of sound in the sub-surface layers.

Sabre sighed into the night, and felt the slow roll of the
swell and Glowchin's body leaning heavily into his. The
big bull remained awake but at peace throughout the
night. Slowly he orientated himself by the stars, and the
sounds and tastes of the sea: old comforting sounds, and
the taste that he had known since the day of his birth: the
taste of home. In the years that had passed he had

travelled thousands of miles, from the frozen wastes in
the north to the cracked west coast of Norway, and
down to the intense heat of the tropics where there was
sand and sun and hot air. He had met swordfish and
sharks, men and their machines; he had spent time with
many friends, and he had lost many. He had been too
close to disaster, and had been plucked from death's grip
by the cow whale who now swam with him. And there
was Glowchin. He had met a blue whale, and had heard
the song of humpbacks; but he knew nothing so well as
the coast of Scotland. His life had begun here, and his
father had been lost here. He had learnt to hunt and to kill
in these waters. Rocked by storms, soothed by the peace
of June, he had been moulded by this coast's character,
and it was to these waters that he would always return.

With the new day, a whisper of wind lifted the seas after
the stillness of the night. Ripple patterns fluttered upon
the sands as the sun climbed higher. A seal played in the
waves, happy and careless, snapping half-heartedly at the
brief flash of an escaping fish. Summer's nonchalance
seduced him into drifting far out across the Sound, where
the water was deep and the tide ran strongly. Suddenly
he froze. He had seen nothing, and at most could have
heard only a sudden burst of sonar, and then no more. He
drew a deep breath, and then slid away and turned for
land. He was scared; frightened by the darkness beneath
him, or by something that waited in the darkness. His
eyes pierced down to where the sun could not reach, far
into the deep blue depths; his ears pierced farther. There
was only the rushing noise of the tide, and the hiss of
light spray above him. But his flippers shot his torpedo
shape landwards, and he did not pause to gasp another

breath; so he never smelt the fresh Scottish air again. Sabre had closed on him from a mile up-current. A brief chirp of sonar had been enough, and then the killer whale had sunk far down into the deep and used the sea's surge to approach his prey. Then he heard the seal bolt for land. He rose and twisted into the light. There was the brown smudge haloed by the silver-gold mirror of the surface. The seal saw him in that same flicker of time, and felt the high-pressure wash of water as the great beast moved in. And then the sun was gone.

Sabre lay there at the surface, numbed by the sudden after-silence of his attack. He called out, and shortly the voices of Spraylash and Glowchin answered him, and he listened to their slow approach. The tide pushed them together in that wide channel. They played and fished through the day, and Sabre paid attention to the sea's voice, but there was nothing that caused him concern, for they were many miles from the navigation lanes of liners and cargo vessels. Here, amongst the tide rips and jagged reefs of kelp-clothed rock, and swirling eddies formed by the islands and the undulating sea floor, few boats ventured, and those that did were only small fishermen drawing lines of lobster pots close to shore. So the Sound belonged to the seals and porpoises, and to the sea birds that flocked here and whitened the faces of the bordering cliffs. For a long time whales had known of this peaceful part of the Scottish coast. Big baleen whales had gulped through the dense blooms of plankton on summer days, and even blue whales had swum here after long ocean migrations. Men had seen them, gushing and spouting, far out over the deep water; so the channel was called Whale Sound.

Sabre's father, Orion, had been born here, and his

father before him, and Sabre himself had been born close by in the Minch, and had visited Whale Sound many times. He had rested from storms beyond the islands; he had hunted here during lean winter months, and he had been at peace here, bathed by the summer sun. And now Spraylash and Glowchin knew of the Sound. Sabre showed them the wrecks in the twilight of the deep, and he rose with them along submarine hills to coral-crusted summits feet beneath the low tide mark. He took them into wide caves beneath the cliffs where conger eels hid, and he swam with them to the many tide-hammered entrances, and across the white-sanded shallows of the Sound's clustered islands. During the nights he took them into areas where the current was weak, and the wind did not reach. When they were not asleep Sabre and Glowchin would stand upright in the calm water, with heads awash, watching the stars make their lazy passage across the night. Their white chins shone in the lunar light, and the dawn would catch them still gazing, as, one by one, the stars winked out. Whale Sound became their home, as it had done for many whales since the end of the last ice-age. It was little different now from when the ice had first receded. The tide had worn caves and passages through the rock, and the dark granite had sanded over until long white bars had formed far out into the channel. Pines marched up the slow mountain slopes, and heather sprouted everywhere. Peat-laden burns washed into the Sound, and white ocean rollers battered at the westernmost islands. Seals and porpoises and whales had arrived beneath other rollers thousands of years earlier, and birds had winged in from the south, chased by the fork-tailed hunters of the air: the falcons. Sea trout had been drawn by the taste of peat in the bays. Whale Sound had burst with life. Constantly enriched with the sea's chemical bounty, life had thrived here ever since.

The killer whales remained in Whale Sound for a month; but on a day at the end of June the sea around them was empty. The animals of the Sound had learnt that the penalty for ignoring the threat of the hunters was death. Nature could spare no more. The high-pitched squeak of porpoise sonar was absent, and the seals had disappeared. Echo-locating could find no fish save the buzzing echoes of dense mackerel shoals. No birds rested on the surface anywhere near the whales: too many had been lost that way. Even the noise of the gulls on the nearby cliffs seemed muted by comparison with the screech-filled air of early June.

It was time to leave, and so during the high tide Sabre led Spraylash and Glowchin through a channel of foaming reefs to the open sea. He took them away from the coast until they felt the character of the water around them change. They passed by flat Hebridean islands to the south, and soon they had a hundred fathoms of water beneath them, and could feel the heavy swell of the North Atlantic drift pushing into their port flanks. More islands lay to their north, but the call of the open ocean drew Sabre towards the west.

Three days after leaving Whale Sound they were fifty miles beyond the Outer Hebrides. They now swam north east, their progress made easy by the warm currents pushing at their tails.

During their brief stay in Whale Sound Spraylash had grown slow and heavy, and Sabre had hunted for her, while Glowchin remained close by her side. Now, as summer passed on the open ocean, as the unbridled

159

winds whipped the tops off the waves and hurled them shoreward, the she-whale barely swam at all, and allowed the tide to carry her at its will. She was not concerned, and only slightly uncomfortable, but she knew that the calf in her swollen belly needed her to rest. Sabre and Glowchin did not urge her on, and were happy to spend their time in the running hills of water, searching for prey, or supporting Spraylash when she grew weak. It would have been easier in the sea-lochs, but there were too many eyes along the shore, and Spraylash would not be able to swim fast if it became necessary. Here, far from land, in the company of the west winds, they would be safe.

The season gradually changed around them. Between the storms, banks of fog smoothed out the sea, and the killer whales found themselves becalmed in the grey September silence. The warm fragrance of autumn hung on the mist, and Spraylash could feel the quickening pulse of the new life within her.

A fast-moving cold front swept down from the north, and piled up against the warm, moist pockets of air on the sleeping ocean. The calm was shattered, and the storm carried away the careless or the weak that lay in its path.

For a time Spraylash was almost unable to swim, and pains rippled through her belly. Sabre swam beneath her, supporting and guiding her through the troughs.

There was one last pain, and in the same moment Sabre was gone, leaving her rolling drunkenly in the sea. On a wind-ravaged seascape he was born: a six-foot bull calf called Thunder. Frantically Spraylash turned and pushed herself through a wave. Amidst the tumbling foam-flecked surface she found them, Sabre and Glowchin, pushing her calf's head and back into the air.

Until it was over they kept him safe from the storm, holding him between them, as they climbed the uncomfortable walls of the rollers all the way to the tall white summits. They fell together down the billowing cascades into the troughs. There they drew deep breaths of the spray-drenched air, before turning to face the next wave.

Four struggling shapes, small against the enormous ugly face of the deep sea.

The front moved southwards, and the waves slowly shrank. Spraylash rolled on to her side, and instinctively the calf homed in for his first meal. She nursed him while the swell became longer and more rhythmic, and patches of blue sky broke the cloud. Sun-bursts patterned the sea, and for a time a sparkling yellow light bathed the killer whales, riding together over the cascading acres of water, towards the broken shallows in the south west.

Sabre, Spraylash and Glowchin feasted on the storm's victims that floated like loose-limbed marionettes in the waves. They found a seal and a pilot whale calf, and as they came closer to the sound of waves pounding against rocky shores, there were the carcasses of sea-birds: many victims of the storm; Nature's excess, that fed the crabs and the fish and the killer whales. Some just fell, rotting, into the abyss, where their substance became part of the ocean that had borne them.

Once again they were four, beginning a winter amongst the islands and deep sounds of the north. Glowchin was no longer a calf, but a fully mature cow, who swam with Thunder whenever he left his mother's side. Glowchin's bulk eclipsed his tiny form as they surged together through the swell. The young cow may have been reminded of the days when she had played with Minch in this same part of the Atlantic, for her frolics with Thunder did not last long, and she would end them by diving deep into the sea, calling out across the great distant chasms of empty ocean. Sabre and Spraylash heard her lonely song, and their replies soothed and comforted her, and called her back; though the voices of her parents were not what she longed to hear.

While Spraylash fed her new calf, Sabre and Glowchin hunted together, their interwoven sonar searching out the cod and herring shoals beginning to swarm in the winter seas. They found little else to prey upon in the tumbling shallows, and as the cold intensified they were forced to scavenge amongst the wrecks, or chase weak, far away echoes, that so often turned out to be a fishing boat or a reef, or the useless, bacteria-worn carcass of a whale, whose warning stench drifted far down the tide.

This was Thunder's nursery, as wild as his name, as cruel as the northern winter could be. Sabre's first months had been the same: he too had spluttered his way through the storms, and felt the tired ache after days of swimming across the wind-lashed deep water, longing for the shelter and peace of island sand-shoals. He too had listened to the sounds of a big bull hunting in the darkness, or calling out protectively to his family on the surface. But there had been crueller times than these: those months alone in the Arctic ice-fields; those times had been lonely, and loneliness was much worse than struggling over a tilting ocean with others of his kind. Even so it was better when the days grew longer, with the sun climbing high into the sky, rather than skating, cold and brief, across the horizon. The North Atlantic drift brought calmer weather, and along the shoreline southern migrants flicked above the cliffs and their chatter hummed on the breeze. Spring's tranquil touch reached into the sea, gradually making existence for the whales something more than scavenging amongst the wrecks, or sheltering in the lee of an island from the snow-laden winds that whistled down from the north. After the blizzards came warm showers, when the killer whales could rest in the calm, feeling the tickle of rain on their backs. Times for Glowchin and Thunder to surf on long white-capped combers, while Sabre and Spraylash were alone together deep in the sea ... Kinder times with the coming of April, and the ocean started to beat with the sounds and promise of life.

Glowchin was now as restless as the Hebridean tides. She hung far behind the others, following at her own speed. She played less with Thunder and grew quiet. At night, while Spraylash and her calf slept, she remained alert, as though listening for voices from far away. It was soothing to allow the swell to bump her body against her mother's, and she felt quite safe with Sabre moving around them, cruising through the gloom; though a great cave of longing had formed in her belly, and she knew that she no longer belonged to these Scottish seas. Neither was her future with her parents. It lay perhaps in the warmer ocean that lapped against the Azores: there, at least, was where the emptiness within her had been seeded.

Her's was not the furious way of the males of her kind, with snarling tons of flesh and bone colliding through the waves, and the weaker or the undetermined bull retreating from the terrifying roar of the master pulsing in its wake. Instead, the hormones within Glowchin, though strong, were infinitely more subtle and sedate.

On her last hunt with Sabre she gorged herself with the squid they had found together, and then hurtled back to the surface, while the bull remained in the deep, killing in the darkness. She found Spraylash, and they spent a few brief moments together before Glowchin called out teasingly to Thunder and sped off into the west. The calf gave chase, but he never caught her, and within minutes the sound of her churning slipstream had diffused into the indecipherable noise of the waves. Thunder never saw his sister again.

The cow swam alone now, against the turbulent currents kicked up by the outer islands. Here she was, midway between the shores of home and the edge of the Continental Shelf, and here she wished to be. When the time came she would be drawn further away from her family, so that she might never meet them again; but when that happened she would not be lonely.

Old Friends and New

A CALL SPREAD OUT across the ocean on the layer of undisturbed water which separates the cold depths from the warmer surface. Here was where the baleens swam on their unhurried travels, and where the voices of whales were borne for hundreds of miles. The call did not belong to a baleen and neither was it the voice of one of man's machines; though it came from far away.

It was so faint that even Spraylash's sensitive ears did not hear it. Sabre slowly turned, listening for the sound to be repeated. He sank down beneath the motion and turbulence of the waves to where the sea was quiet. For many minutes he listened. A high whistle from above broke the spell. Spraylash was calling, concerned by the bull's strange behaviour. Had he heard the sounds of danger? Sabre rose silently and nudged gently into her side. He knew what he had heard, and he understood what it meant.

Slowly he swam, with Spraylash and Thunder behind him, towards the sunrise. From the east his destiny had called. No further sound beckoned him on, but he swam with a sureness of his direction: hills, smouldering orange in the dawn light, appeared above the horizon in their path.

Morning drew on, and the water became shallower. Sabre had not veered from his course, and had maintained

165

a slow pace towards the coast. Several times he echo-
located, and each time all three whales heard the return
wave of a large body approaching. When it was very
close Sabre was silent. He stopped and waited.

Then a note sounded, louder and louder, until it filled
the sea and Sabre knew to what creature that voice
belonged. The note died away and left an ominous quiet,
as an enormous grey shape materialised in front of Sabre
and his family. The body was terribly scarred, and the
skin was cracked and old. The mouth was almost tooth-
less, and the eyes were dull. Pushing the whale on was a
great round tail, split and torn, which, when it came to
rest, hung limply, betraying the many years and many
miles that it had driven the huge beast across the Atlantic's wastes: and perhaps the most distinctive feature of
all was the whale's colossal dorsal fin, smashed, bent, and
riven in two.

Forkfin and Sabre stared at each other, as they had
done when the younger of the two had been a mere calf.
Years and adventures were now between them, and
much had happened since Sabre's time in the Great
School, but the lessons and the memory of friends, and
the long journeys, could never be forgotten. Forkfin had
taught Sabre many things, and above all how to lead.
Now the old giant was dying. Indeed he had seemed too
old all those years ago; and yet he had been indomitable,
possessed of great power.

The fires were almost burnt out, and the old body
appeared poised to fall into the ocean's deep. Somehow
Forkfin had survived this long. His strength had lasted
up to the previous evening. He had brought the Great
School on a journey that had lasted three months, from
the tropics to the coast of Scotland. He had maintained

command long enough to reach Sabre's home waters. Finally his strength had failed, and three young bulls had cast him out, and assumed between them a command that was doomed even as it started. The Great School was in danger of breaking up, for none of the three bulls was strong enough, or old enough, to assume total leadership. Forkfin swam off, calling and searching for the one whale he knew could master the School. His one last quest, and now, with Sabre before him, he had succeeded.

Spraylash and her calf remained silent and overawed by the great grey whale. No sound passed between Sabre and Forkfin. Neither was there any need for sound, for each knew what lay in the future. Forkfin understood that his task was over, and Sabre realised that his was just beginning.

After several minutes Forkfin's foreflippers began to move, and his tail lifted. His grey bulk turned slowly, sleepily, until he faced the direction from which he had appeared. Again his tail wafted upwards, and the old whale moved off. Sabre swam at his side, while Spraylash and Thunder followed, bewildered, some distance behind.

In the end the Great One had as much dignity as in the days when he was Master of his School. It must have been hard for him to die, for he of all beasts had the most tenacious grip on life. Too often in the past he had swum in death's slipstream: in the Arctic where ice had finished everything he loved; in Norway where men had taken everything he had learned to love again, and in his many battles from the northern pack-ice to the heat-swollen African coast, where so often he had had to fight for those in his care.

And now that he was about to die he was not alone. He swam his last painful mile not with the Great School, but with a whale he had known so long ago, one who would now have to take over for him. Sabre was with him at the finish, and if the old bull could want anything, he could ask for nothing more than to end his life in such a way.

Side by side the two giant shadows slid across the peaceful sea. They slowed and stopped, and hung there, tilting slightly in the tide. A presence hovered in that place, and an understanding greater than any language could express. Then the Great One dropped silently away, until his grey shape merged into the nebulous anonymity of the Atlantic's deep. It was finished, but the presence and understanding remained with that other vast shape, motionless on the surface.

Another lost friend.

They left in silence, Sabre leading them up the coast in the direction Forkfin had pointed. That way lay his future: the Great School, Sabre's responsibility now. He must find them and master them, and when he had done that he would have to care for them until he was no longer capable of the task. Some would recognise him and some would not. The young bulls who now led the School would try to scare him off. He would have to send them away to make their own lives in the wide ocean, like Forkfin had done to him all that time ago. That would be the easy part; fighting. What would not be so easy was the command; controlling and pulling the School together, as Forkfin had shown him. The trust would come slowly, depending on how well he led them. But there would be company for Spraylash and

Thunder, and while there were no sounds of propellers in the sea he could watch the calves play on the surf-tipped banks of the long Atlantic swell.

Piercing sonar noises came to their ears from the north. They had found the Great School: a hungry fragmenting pack of sea-wolves emptying the sea around them with their hunting cries. They would be easy to approach, and then he would shock them into silence. The initiative was his from the beginning, and if he ever lost it he might lose much more. He called to Spraylash and Thunder to follow, and then sped off towards the calls.

He shot into their midst from below, his colossal bulk hurtling past them up to the surface, through a wave and into the air. Beneath a silver veil he crashed back into the sea and allowed the bubbles to settle, while the killer-whales surrounding him grew silent, staring at his awesome size. Their eyes took in his huge form, with his dark back etched by the scars of years. They saw the brilliant flame marks on his belly and flanks, the tall weapon on his back, and the big curved flippers and flukes. His eyes caught theirs and held their stare, and they recognised him for what he was: their leader.

There were two bulls who would not at first accept the new Master. Blinded by the hormones in their bodies they rushed towards him, screaming and furious. But Sabre had anticipated the careless attack, and dispatched them with the ease of one used to fighting.

A third bull, the largest of the three who had exiled Forkfin, did not attack Sabre. He watched the quick explosive battle with the other two, and then merely stared at the big bull, before turning and swimming away. He was the dangerous one, the one who might one day return: bigger and stronger, and with more understanding. The two beaten bulls, one trailing a plume of blood, followed him into the distance. It was done. Sabre was Master of the Great School.

The three bulls would stay together for a little while, perhaps for a year, but the first cows they met would drive them into snarling argument. Perhaps in a few days the strong one would leave the other two and make his own way across the sea, or he might stay and teach them how to survive and thrive without dependence upon the School.

For Sabre the future was more certain. From this moment on, every whale in the Great School would depend on him for leadership and control. If he failed he could lose them all. Forkfin himself had lost his first pod to the whale gunners in a Norwegian fjord. Sabre had escaped the whalers once, and he knew what sounds to listen for, but there were other dangers: angry sperm whales whose jaws could break an adult killer in half; squid and dangerous wrecks on the sea floor that could hold a whale until it drowned; sharks and storms; reefs and shallows, deadly in an ebbing tide ... Too many dangers, and he would have to be alert for them all.

He swam among his wards, touching them or listening to their voices as he passed by. Some of the cows he recognised, though a few of them, and all the calves, were new. Then he found the one he knew must be there. Old and tired, surrounded by friends, Nightshadow looked at the big bull, whom she had delivered and cared for in this very corner of the Atlantic. They had lost Orion here, and now Forkfin; and they had forgotten little that had passed, though much had become a cloud of memory rather than sharp distinct images, for there was a great deal to remember. The first voice that Sabre ever heard now came to his ears again, as soft and comforting, as gentle and personal, as it had always been, so that this huge bull could imagine himself a calf once more, six feet instead of thirty, with a little hooked dorsal instead of the tall straight fin, baffled by his bubble-filled world.

A silence swept over the entire School as the Great One and Nightshadow met, speaking of things that only they could understand. It is possible that the killers could not speak of things that had happened long ago, that their language was designed only for the needs of the present, and that much of the past was a very hazy memory, for the ocean's element is a harsh one, which might not afford the luxury of afterthought other than of the most traumatic experience; but it is very likely that these two large animals had as much understanding, with as much feeling, as could be implied by the size and complexity of their brains.

Soon Spraylash arrived, with her awe-struck calf close in to her side. Like Sabre she swam among the School, touching, and emitting her own soft calls of friendship: from the beginning her presence was welcome.

The story is told, but not complete. Sabre might well live to be as old as Forkfin, leading his School across the wide Atlantic; killing and moving on, playing and sleeping and surfing on big growling breakers; and moving on. But tomorrow a whaler might find him and send a harpoon into his skull, or he might lead his pod on to some sandy shallows, where a fast ebbing tide would leave them all to the mercy of the sun. Dangers are rife on the deep sea; though the biggest menace must be humankind.

171

Whale

The waves lapped against the many backs that
breached the surface. Evening began to set in as the warm
ocean breeze died to almost nothing. In the west the sun
was sinking behind a low-lying island. Gulls flew overhead, catching the last warming rays. To the east the
mainland stood out above the sea, proud and promising,
red and deep crimson in the dwindling light. All of
Scotland, with her heather moors and her blushing
mountains and her deep, still lochs, fell to the peaceful
spell of a summer evening. From somewhere, a long way
out to sea, came a soft sound, almost lost above the slow
surge of the waves. In that moment a long bow-wave
furrowed the surface, and a massive fin lifted imperiously into the air. A call rang out, and the sea was suddenly
chaotic and swollen as the whales spouted. The bow-
wave rolled towards the north, up the mainland towards
Cape Wrath. Then out of disorder came a fluid controlled
movement, as the killers set off in the wake of the big
bull.

All at once there were many fins in the air, curling and
cutting back into the smooth water. Harsh dark outlines,
blotched here and there with white, moved beneath the
silvery puffs of the whale blows. A crescendo of noise
shook the air as the lungs of each whale expelled their
stale air. The whole fluid sequence was over as the last
hooked fin rolled beneath the surface. Then, half a mile
beyond where the last whale had blown, the tall fin
flashed momentarily, and a huge form moved across the
curve-faced wall of a building Atlantic roller. The fin fell
away, and the swirl settled to the contoured pattern of
the waves. The stealthily moving shadow became a part
of the deep-down darkness of the sea, and was lost
against that darkness: the killer whale was gone.

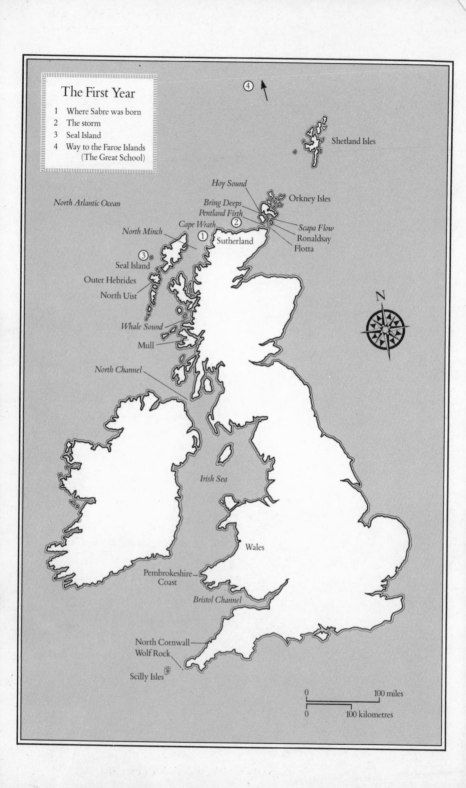

The First Year

1 Where Sabre was born
2 The storm
3 Seal Island
4 Way to the Faroe Islands
 (The Great School)

Shetland Isles

Hoy Sound

North Atlantic Ocean

Bring Deeps
Pentland Firth

Orkney Isles

Cape Wrath

North Minch

Sutherland

Scapa Flow
Ronaldsay
Flotta

Seal Island

Outer Hebrides

North Uist

N

Whale Sound

Mull

North Channel

Irish Sea

Wales

Pembrokeshire
Coast

Bristol Channel

North Cornwall
Wolf Rock

Scilly Isles

0   100 miles

0   100 kilometres